Access to Information
and Social Justice

ACCESS TO INFORMATION AND SOCIAL JUSTICE

Critical Research Strategies for Journalists, Scholars, and Activists

Edited by Jamie Brownlee
and Kevin Walby

ARP BOOKS · WINNIPEG, MANITOBA

ARP Books (Arbeiter Ring Publishing)
201E-121 Osborne Street
Winnipeg, Manitoba
Canada R3L 1Y4
arpbooks.org

Cover by Michael Carroll
Typeset by Relish New Brand Experience
Printed in Canada by Friesens on paper from 100% post-consumer waste.

ARP Books acknowledges the generous support of the Manitoba Arts Council and
the Canada Council for the Arts for our publishing program. We acknowledge the
financial support of the Government of Canada through the Canada Book Fund and
the Province of Manitoba through the Book Publishing Tax Credit and the Book
Publisher Marketing Assistance Program of Manitoba Culture, Heritage, and Tourism.

CONTENTS

FOREWORD vii
   Robert Cribb

INTRODUCTION Access to Information and Social Justice in Canada 1
   Jamie Brownlee and Kevin Walby

CHAPTER 1 Seeking Truth from Power: Strategies for Using Access Laws 21
   Dean Jobb

CHAPTER 2 The Power of Numbers: Holding Governments Accountable
   with Their Own Data 34
   Leslie Young

CHAPTER 3 Four Barriers to Access to Information: Perspectives
   of a Frequent User 53
   Jeffrey Monaghan

CHAPTER 4 Using Access to Information to Separate Oil and State
   in Canada 75
   Keith Stewart and Kyla Tanner

CHAPTER 5 Games "Bureaucats" Play 94
   Franke James

CHAPTER 6 Peeking Behind the Curtain: Accessing the Backstage
   of Security Intelligence Threat Assembly 133
   Alex Luscombe and Michael-Anthony Lutfy

CHAPTER 7   ATI/FOI Records and Prison Expansion in Canada: How to Get the Word Out   149
Justin Piché

CHAPTER 8   Beyond ATIP: New Methods for Researching State Surveillance Practices   161
Christopher Parsons

AFTERWORD   Helpful Tips from Frequent ATI/FOI Users   184
CONTRIBUTORS   189
ACKNOWLEDGEMENTS   194

FOREWORD

Robert Cribb

The mistreatment of children in daycare centres. Public health risks from dangerous prescription drugs. Scientific research into climate change and environmental degradation. Questionable public spending by elected officials. These are all important matters of public interest documented inside filing cabinets and computer hard drives in government offices across Canada. Those records contain essential truths that inform how we live our lives, how we are protected by public policy and how governments act in our name. Those records are the lifeblood of democratic debate, public education, and legislative reform. And they are, all too frequently, hidden from us.

In Canada, information laws exist to protect our collective right to access public records. But there is a moment that unfolds in many quests for government records when the information seeker—be they researcher, journalist, academic, or citizen—encounters a bureaucratic fortification. Government transparency in Canada, inspired by noble legal concepts such as "freedom of information" and "access to information," is frequently defined more by an unspoken code of silence that undermines those ideas. Indeed, there is a vast chasm between principle and practice where freedom of information in concerned. "The overarching purpose of access to information legislation is to facilitate democracy by helping to ensure that citizens have the information required to participate meaningfully in the democratic process and that politicians and bureaucrats remain accountable to the citizenry," as former Supreme Court of Canada Justice Gérard LaForest famously wrote in a 1997 decision (LaForest, Gérard V., *Dagg v. Canada* 1997). The poetic resonance of that idea is lost, however, when a simple record request is assessed with a 100-day time delay, or thousands of dollars in processing fees, justified with confounding and often indefensible rhetoric.

As a frequent user of federal as well as provincial information laws in my work as an investigative reporter, I have come to view the 30-day legislated time frame for government response to information requests as whimsical fancy. I'm far from alone. Too often, extensions run into months and sometimes years. In an infamous 2014 case, Canada's Department of National Defence claimed a 1,110-day time extension in order to respond to an access request (Office of the Information Commissioner of Canada 2014). Tested in appeals, these self-claimed government extensions frequently fail the test of legitimacy. Yet the process of formally challenging unreasonable delays can take months. Even after the wait, insult often looms due to outrageous fee assessments and other complications.

Canada, once an access to information leader, has fallen badly behind thanks to legislative neglect and what often feels like open bureaucratic contempt for public accountability. A 2012 international study of freedom of information laws in 89 countries placed Canada 57th in the world behind Mongolia, Indonesia, and Honduras (Centre for Law and Democracy 2012). "As a country that was once among the world's leaders in government openness, it is unfortunate that Canada has dropped so far down the list," says an analysis accompanying the rankings. The authors blame Canada's "antiquated approach to access to information," which includes "lax timelines, imposition of access fees, lack of a proper public interest override, and blanket exemptions for certain political offices," all of which "contravene international standards." It cites another, more systemic, cause for concern: a "lack of political will to improve the situation." Despite repeated calls for a legislative overhaul of Canada's three-decade-old *Access to Information Act*, there has been no serious consideration along these lines.

Instead, there has been continued deterioration. Recently, the Canadian federal information commissioner issued a verbal throwing up of hands at the growing inability of her office to protect the interests of Canadian information seekers. The combination of a growing number of complaints from requesters—which increased by 30 percent in 2013-14 alone—and a nine percent funding cut since 2009 has strained resources to a point that will "jeopardize her ability to safeguard the rights conferred by the *Access to Information Act*" (Office of the Information Commissioner of Canada 2014: 37).

The tools of government secrecy are also getting sharper. While denials, delays, and high fees remain the tried and true techniques of non-disclosure, the arsenal of information suppression has expanded to include the systematic destruction of (or "failure to maintain") records that could trigger public controversy. Most simply, there's the "don't write it down" strategy, an astute means of undermining accountability by neglecting to create records in the first place. As a former director of access to information and privacy for the federal Immigration and Refugee Board told me candidly, "at first, you'd have minutes being kept for executive meetings. Once they were asked for [by the public] they died down until they disappeared and nobody kept minutes at all." These strategic changes in internal record-keeping protocol are founded upon a deep culture of entitlement, he said. "Several senior people have said to me quite bluntly … 'What right does the public have to know? We run things our way.'" Listening to insiders speak about the machinations of government transparency over the past two decades, it is clear to me that the popular notion of a public service acting as custodian of the public interest is an outdated legend.

To be sure, there are civil servants who take their duty to assist the public seriously. But a growing body of academic evidence, public disclosures, and the outcomes of hundreds of requests I've filed across the country over two and a half decades paint the picture of a public service that too often acts with impunity and contempt. Consider, for example, the expanding black hole of government records that has emerged through the widespread use of instant messaging communications. Instant messaging by government officials has put millions of records, many of them essential to understanding how decisions are made on our behalf, beyond the reach of most Canadians. The clearest illustration unfolded recently in Canada Revenue Agency (CRA) emails that were made public. The emails showed that the agency had destroyed all text message records of its employees and stopped logging them for future reference—a quietly executed decision that effectively removed the ability of citizens to access the communications of federal employees in one of the country's most important ministries. "BBM and SMS are no longer logged and previous logs have been deleted," reads an email confirming the move in August 2014. The response from a CRA deputy minister comes the next day: "Excellent. Thanks so much for your prompt action!" (De Souza 2014). Of course, the CRA is far from alone. A 2013 review of eleven federal ministries by the federal information commissioner found that instant messaging among political decision-makers poses the "real risk that information that should be accessible by requesters is being irremediably deleted or lost" (Legault 2013: 3).

Perhaps even more scandalous is the outright destruction of records. Recently, a controversial scrapping of two gas-fired power plants in Ontario (at a cost of $1.1 billion in public funds) triggered stunning police allegations that government officials paid $10,000 to have records detailing their decisions erased from government computers (Ferguson and Brennan 2014; Morrow 2014). A special investigation into the email disappearances by the province's information and privacy commissioner concluded that it "strains credulity" to assert that no records were retained as part of such a significant public policy decision. "It is difficult to accept that the routine deletion of emails was not in fact an attempt by staff in the former Minister's office to avoid transparency and accountability in relation to their work," the report concludes (Cavoukian 2013: 1-2).

Together with record destruction in the secrecy toolbox sits the altering of documents prior to release. While it has long been an issue of great suspicion among those who are frequent users of federal as well as provincial information laws, there have been rare moments when this practice has been exposed. In October 2014, a freedom of information request filed by a *Toronto Star* reporter seeking details of public school board expenses filed by trustees exposed allegations of document tampering. According to an internal email by the freedom of information coordinator, the documents were tainted by "misinformation" and "trustee tampering" (Rushowy 2014). While the incident triggered an immediate investigation by the province's information and privacy commissioner, there are currently no legislative consequences for failing to properly maintain records, or even for the willful destruction of records under Ontario's freedom of information laws.

We should not be surprised by any of this. Self-preservation is an evolved government instinct. Back in 2001, Canada's former Auditor General, Denis Desautels, flagged the country's burgeoning secrecy code when he observed: "There is a reluctance to let Parliament and the public know how government programs are working, because if things are going badly you may be giving your opponents the stick to beat you with" (Desautels 2001: 86). Understanding how that sentiment plays out behind the scenes holds stark insights. Following a lengthy battle with an Ontario ministry (for records that I eventually won on appeal) I obtained, through a follow-up request, the internal ministry documents created as part of that negotiation. They contained a glimpse into the state of mind of those who quietly throw up roadblocks to prevent the release of records. The departmental communications explicitly referred to my request as "contentious" and identified me as "a member of the media." Internal memos discussing their response to the request had headlines such as "What We're Facing," and included a lengthy analysis of how to limit public relations damage from the disclosure. According to internal Ontario Ministry of Training, Colleges and Universities correspondence, obtained through a freedom of information request, these strategies included circulating stories to "key ethnic media" and having the minister do interviews on television to explain legislation and its "benefits." The prevailing tone throughout is reminiscent of a military siege mentality as opposed to civic responsibility.

Despite occasional revelations and momentary outrages, there remains little public concern about government secrecy in Canada. Cases of obstinate information denials or delays that would trigger scandals in the United States often inspire little more than a knowing sigh from Canadians. A steady string of opposition politicians have railed against the scourge of government information concealment and the need for legislative change. Yet these same politicians, when they find themselves in power, tend to run from the public accountability they once hailed. Indeed, most political leaders in Canada have come to realize a distinctly Canadian truth: government openness is not an issue that garners votes. It's a high-risk, low-reward political proposition. In the 2006 election campaign, Stephen Harper's Conservative government made access to information an election platform issue, promising changes that would heighten transparency and accountability. Nearly a decade later, the prevailing sentiment among users of the law is that the challenges to access have never been greater.

In the end, government secrecy in Canada remains a big problem. That's why this book matters. It's time for a thoughtful national debate on the legislative mechanisms designed to empower us all to seek answers. It's time to expand public awareness about how the right to know is being deliberately undermined, often with smug condescension, in ways that centralize power through the control of information. Evidence, data, and illustrative anecdotes, collected in one place, are needed to move this debate beyond the traditional he-said-she-said mush of inaction and toward a shared acknowledgement of the need for change. It is my hope that this book marks that beginning.

REFERENCES

Cavoukian, A. 2013. Deleting Accountability: Records Management Practices of Political Staff. Office of the Information and Privacy Commissioner, June 5, 2013.

Centre for Law and Democracy. 2012. Global Right to Information Rating. At

Desautels, D. 2001. Reflections on a Decade of Serving Parliament. Report of the Auditor General of Canada to the House of Commons, February.

De Souza, M. 2014. CRA Trashed All Records of Staff Messages. *Toronto Star*, December 23.

Ferguson, R. and R. Brennan. 2014. Liberals Paid $10,000 to Wipe Computers. *Toronto Star*, December 19.

Legault, S. 2013. Access to Information at Risk from Instant Messaging, Special Report to Parliament, November.

Morrow, A. 2014. McGuinty's Top Adviser Told Aides How to Erase E-mails. *The Globe and Mail*, December 19.

Office of the Information Commissioner of Canada. 2014. Annual Report 2013-2014. Ottawa.

Rushowy, K. 2014. Trustees Tampered with FOI Request for Expense Reports, Emails Suggest. *Toronto Star*, October 16.

LEGAL CASES

LaForest, Gerard V., Dagg v. Canada (Minister of Finance), 1997 2 SCR 403.

ACCESS TO INFORMATION AND SOCIAL JUSTICE IN CANADA

Jamie Brownlee and Kevin Walby

U nder Canadian law, every citizen has the right to request information from federal, provincial/territorial, and municipal governments. All orders of government are subject to the protocols set out in the *Access to Information Act* (ATIA) at the federal level and Freedom of Information (FOI) legislation at the provincial/territorial and municipal levels. These legal mechanisms allow individuals to request information from government agencies and to review records, policy documents, and correspondence that show how these agencies operate. With this information, we can tell a different story about government practices and decision-making than we can when we rely solely on what is available in the public domain. This is because data gathered using Access to Information (ATI) and FOI requests is different in kind than the open-source material found on government websites, the rhetorical speeches of politicians, and the sanitized information packages of public relations firms. It is information that illustrates how power operates in democratic societies, exposes the often secretive dealings between state and corporate elites, and is critical to developing resistance strategies and promoting social justice.

Not only does access to information underpin society's most important democratic ideals—including government accountability, freedom of expression, and freedom of the press—but many international organizations now characterize access to information as a fundamental human right (Bishop 2012). In the wake of the high-profile National Security Agency (NSA) scandals in the US, and globally through the ongoing debates on the WikiLeaks exposures and the Edward Snowden affair, it is clear that access to information is an increasingly pressing issue.

For over three decades, ATI and FOI protocols have been valuable research tools for Canadian journalists. However, these protocols also support the work of scholars, civil libertarians, and public interest researchers. *Access to Information and Social Justice: Critical Research Strategies for Journalists, Scholars, and Activists* brings together essays by academics, social activists, journalists, and other justice advocates on the role of, and challenges to, access to information in Canada today. This volume contributes to a growing international literature on the politics of information (e.g., Buckley et al. 2013; Cordis and Warren 2014; Holsen and Pasquier 2011; Pike 2005; Savage and Hyde 2014; Suthar 2011; Worthy 2013) by exploring a series of interrelated topics on the policy, politics, and practice of access to information in the Canadian context. These include how ATI and FOI protocols originated and have changed; how government employees manage and control information; how access to information investigations have been used to uncover the covert activities of state security agencies; how the material obtained through ATI/FOI requests has informed a number of key public policy debates (e.g., tar sands development and prison expansion); how document leaks and whistleblowers are treated under the *Security of Information Act*; how "exemption clauses" in access to information legislation permit governments to keep information secret; and how the media and the public respond to ATI/FOI-generated data. In addition to documenting some of the most important political stories that have come to light through ATI/FOI requests, one of the goals of *Access to Information and Social Justice* is to provide practical tips, guidance, and strategic advice about how to conduct access to information research.

Access to Information Research in Canada: Real Successes

ATI/FOI requests are being used more frequently as a way to gather information in Canada. According to Treasury Board statistics, ATI requests at the federal level increased by 43 percent between 2006 and 2011 (McKie 2012). In 2010, federal government departments and agencies received over 35,000 ATI requests (*CBC News* 2011). With this growing interest has come an increasing number of successes, defined here as instances where the public has become aware of an event or issue because of information uncovered through these kinds of investigations. Stanley Tromp (2010), freedom of information caucus coordinator of the Canadian Association of Journalists, has compiled a list of news stories that were made possible through information requests filed under Canada's ATIA between 2006 and 2010. Here is a sample from Tromp:

· 2007. "Federal auditors are targeting some of the biggest names in corporate Canada for allegedly overcharging millions of dollars in their contracts with government, heavily censored records released through the ATIA showed" (p. 34).

· 2007. "Canada was cast as a bad actor that aggressively campaigned alongside countries with tarnished human rights records in its failed bid to derail the United Nations Declaration on the Rights of Indigenous Peoples ... documents released to Amnesty International under the ATIA show that the government fought against the declaration despite advice from its own officials" (p. 31).

· 2007. "Canada's nuclear safety watchdog appears to be too cozy with the industry it's supposed to monitor, suggests an independent report obtained under the ATIA. The study ordered by the Canadian Nuclear Safety Commission cites long-standing complaints that the regulator focuses far more on the companies it licenses than on concerned lobby groups or citizens" (p. 13).

- 2007. "Three out of four suspects stun-gunned by the RCMP were unarmed, according to a review of 563 cases that shows Tasers are often used for compliance rather than to defuse major threats ... Statistics were released through the *ATIA*" (p. 20).
- 2008. "The Canadian government strongly opposed tougher U.S. rules to prevent listeria and lobbied the United States to accept Canada's more lenient standards, internal documents released through the *ATIA* reveal" (p. 1).
- 2008. "A report commissioned [by Health Canada] from outside consultants warned that the country's main consumer-protection law, the 1969 *Hazardous Products Act*, was seriously outdated and woefully inadequate to safeguard the public from perils in everyday products. The report was obtained through the *ATIA*" (p. 3).
- 2008. "The federal government was warned years ago by its own experts that climate change was threatening critical infrastructure across the country, putting human health and the economy in jeopardy, reveal newly-released federal reports obtained by Canwest News Service" (p. 7).
- 2008. "The RCMP used taxpayers' dollars to hire researchers to author papers that undermine Insite, the supervised injection site in Vancouver opposed by the Mounties and the Conservative government. Pivot Legal Society, an advocacy group working on behalf of the poor and dispossessed, made the discovery through an *ATIA* request" (p. 18).
- 2009. "An award-winning 'BPA-free' baby bottle contained the highest traces of the toxic chemical when Health Canada tested for leaching into water ... The test results surprised Health Canada scientists involved, according to records released under the *ATIA*" (p. 5).
- 2009. "The Maple Leaf plant at the centre of the deadly listeriosis outbreak wasn't properly monitoring and recording the cleaning of its meat slicing equipment earlier in the year,

federal inspection records reveal ... Canadian Food Inspection Agency records for the facility, obtained by The Canadian Press under the *ATIA*, show on-site inspectors highlighted problems with the company's slicer sanitation processes some six months before the outbreak" (p. 9).

· 2009. "Pollution will continue to plague Alberta's oil sands despite plans to pipe harmful greenhouse gases deep underground, according to documents obtained by the Toronto Star through the *ATIA* ... chemicals linked to acid rain, respiratory problems and ozone depletion could escape into the atmosphere at an even faster rate, thanks to an estimated tripling of production from one million barrels a day in 2007 to 3.4 million barrels a day in 2017" (p. 11).

· 2009. "The Canadian Forces needs to step up its supervision of training facilities and family centres on bases across the country, according to a military police investigation that found a disproportionate number of sexual assault cases involved young people at the hands of older personnel" (p. 17).

· 2010. "Citizenship and Immigration Minister Jason Kenney blocked any reference to gay rights in a new study guide for immigrants applying for Canadian citizenship ... Internal documents show an early draft of the guide contained sections noting that homosexuality was decriminalized in 1969; that the Charter of Rights and Freedoms forbids discrimination based on sexual orientation; and that same-sex marriage was legalized nationally in 2005. But Kenney, who fought same-sex marriage when it was debated in Parliament, ordered those key sections removed" (p. 28).

· 2010. "Health Canada documents obtained through an *ATIA* request reveal close to 250 internal incidents [at Canada's National Microbiology Lab in Winnipeg] ... were reported in the lab between 2005 and 2009. The incidents range in severity and include benign finger cuts, potential exposures to chemicals and viruses such as avian influenza, and equipment failures in Level 3 and 4 containment labs" (p. 6).

In more recent years, ATI investigations have continued to inform newsmaking on a diverse range of public interest issues. Early in 2014, documents obtained by the John Howard Society of Canada revealed that inmates with acute mental illnesses were being locked up in prolonged isolation and "grossly inadequate" conditions in Canadian mental health facilities (Harris 2014). These exposures came two years after the Canadian Human Rights Commission argued in a report to the United Nations Committee Against Torture that Canada should prohibit the use of solitary confinement for persons with mental illness. Also in 2014, a CBC news investigation unearthed a 2011 report about a TransCanada gas pipeline rupture in northern Alberta. The investigation showed that the report had been intentionally suppressed by federal regulators, likely due to government concerns about TransCanada's negotiation of the contentious Keystone XL Pipeline proposal (Hildebrandt 2014). This disclosure is relevant in light of two other recent ATI exposés. The first involved data obtained from the National Energy Board (NEB) showing that the rate of safety-related incidents on federally regulated pipelines doubled during the 2000s, while the rate of reported spills and leaks increased threefold (Hildebrandt 2013). The second was a series of documents detailing over 9,000 environmental violations in the tar sands since 1996, and the fact that less than one percent of these infractions have been subject to any prosecution (Weber 2013).

Equally troubling was the discovery that the federal government has been spying on anti-tar sands activists as well as Indigenous and environmental organizations across Canada (Millar 2013). These are groups that the government considers to be its "adversaries," a fact that was also brought to light through documents obtained under access to information legislation (Fitzpatrick 2012). At the root of the story is that the government created a domestic "intelligence and surveillance" program involving a broad-based alliance between the NEB's security team, the Canadian Security and Intelligence Service (CSIS), the RCMP, officials from the TransCanada and Enbridge corporations, and a private security contractor hired by the NEB. The underlying purpose of this alliance was to monitor dissent and manage information to support framing federal strategies on proposed energy projects as successful, rather than solely focused on servicing Big Oil. In response, the BC Civil Liberties Association developed a new online tool to help citizens file ATI requests on themselves to determine if authorities were monitoring them. The new website offers templates for personal information requests to federal departments, including the RCMP, CSIS, the NEB, and National Resources Canada (Ball 2014, https://bccla.org/dont-spy-on-me/10388-2/).

These examples illustrate the value of ATI/FOI research for investigative journalism. At the same time, ATI/FOI research is increasingly relevant in academia. Both editors of this volume, for example, have incorporated access to information requests in their academic research. In his research on the corporatization of Canadian universities, Jamie Brownlee (2015a; 2015b) used FOI requests to expose the transformation of academic labour in Ontario and the increasing reliance on contract or part-time faculty. Previous efforts to obtain these data had frustrated Canadian researchers. In 2004, a similar study tried to gather the same information using FOI requests but—in part because universities were not subject to the *Freedom of Information and Protection of Privacy Act* (FIPPA) at that time—most universities did not provide the data (Ontario Confederation of University Faculty Associations 2004). To address this gap, in 2010 Brownlee sent FOI requests to eighteen universities in Ontario, all of which had been added under the FIPPA legislation. His data confirmed that universities are, indeed, increasingly relying on temporary contract faculty. It also revealed that the lack of public information about this trend is not because university administrators are *unable* to provide the data (as they so often claimed), it is because they have been *unwilling* to do so unless compelled by legislation.

Similarly, Kevin Walby has used ATI research to explore issues in policing and security in Canada. Jeffrey Monaghan and Walby (2012) used federal ATI law to document how "threat" classifications and categories are constructed within Canadian policing and intelligence agencies. Targeting requests at the CSIS Integrated Threat Assessment Centre, Monaghan and Walby received 25 intelligence reports, some of which included reference to "Multi-Issue Extremism" or "MIE," a category employed by CSIS that groups "terrorism, extremism and activism into an aggregate threat matrix" (p. 134). In other words, CSIS has come to construe non-violent social movement groups, such as environmentalist and Indigenous activists, as MIEs or as national security threats. Another example is Walby's work on the policing of the Occupy movement in Ottawa. More and more, conservation officers are involved in policing work in cities. Alex Luscombe and Walby (2014) used ATI requests to uncover links between conservation officers, the RCMP, and CSIS, the latter two of which included conservation officers within their classified loops of intelligence reporting. Conservation officers worked daily with police to disrupt the mobilizations, and coordinated with other security agencies as well. The 2,000 pages of internal documents received from the conservation agency (the National Capital Commission) showed that the Commission operates like a state policing agency, and has been coordinating with intelligence agencies and private stakeholders across Canada.

Using ATI-based information to shape public debates in this way is critical, given the limitations of relying on other methods to access insider information. For instance, when WikiLeaks first began releasing large swathes of government documents, many proponents celebrated the move as ushering in a new era of radical transparency and hacktivist democracy. Yet, as Alasdair Roberts (2012) and others have argued, there are a number of problems with this approach. For one, disclosure itself is often not enough. Further, not a lot was done with the WikiLeaks disclosures because of the immense amount of material that was released, and the difficulties in assembling and disseminating the information in a way that would galvanize public attention. Aside from a few prominent exposures that went viral, the public remained largely unaware of the contents of the information, and governments were able to work to quickly repress the organization.

These successes show how ATI/FOI research can be used to make Canadians aware of important social justice issues. This volume expands on and provides additional examples from a number of journalists, activists, and researchers in Canada. Highlighting both their unique experiences and some of the common challenges they face in doing this kind of work, the contributions illustrate how access to information research has been used to expose the most important political issues of the day, ranging from energy policy and climate change, to prison expansion, state surveillance, and security intelligence. At a more practical level, the authors highlight many of the key shortcomings of Canada's ATI laws and protocols, as well some of the strategies that can be used to overcome them. As discussed throughout *Access to Information and Social Justice*, there are many problems with Canada's access to information regime, especially given the changes in government policies that have taken shape since September 11, 2001.

Canada's ATI Regime: Current Challenges

Canada's federal *Access to Information Act* (*ATIA*) came into effect in 1983. At the time, the *ATIA* was characterized as a groundbreaking initiative that placed Canada among a small group of progressive nations with respect to the right of citizens to access government information. While the *ATIA* may have been "cutting edge" 30 years ago, it has yet to be updated and, as a result, the Canadian ATI regime has "fallen behind" from an international perspective (Beeby 2011; Bronskill 2015; Chase 2011; Tromp 2008). According to a cross-national study of freedom of information legislation by the Centre for Law and Democracy (2013), on a number of measures, such as the scope of Canada's ATI legislation (e.g., the number of excluded agencies and the capacity of governments to evade the laws), Canada ranks near the bottom. Nearly all of the 95 countries under review—with the exceptions of Australia, Iceland, China, Greece, and Tajikistan—made more government information available to their citizens than Canada.

The rankings established by the Centre for Law and Democracy also show that Canada performs especially poorly in the "exceptions and refusals" category. This category measures how often information is withheld and under what circumstances. The Centre's results highlight that Canada's *ATIA* contains a broad list of exceptions, including several that are not based on preventing harm. A related problem is exemption and redaction, or the removal of information from government documents prior to release. For example, there are blanket exemptions for certain political offices. Any time that information involves the work of a minister's office or a cabinet decision, it can be withheld. In the current political climate, more and more documents are claimed to be a matter of cabinet or ministerial confidence, and some government bodies, like the Prime Minister's Office and the Privy Council Office, are not subject to ATI laws at all. Questions have been raised about "creative avoidance" by governments, such as whether government agencies are deliberately using these measures as a loophole to allow for non-disclosure (e.g., inviting someone from the minister's office to meetings so that the proceedings are subject to ministerial confidence) (Jiwani and Krawchenko 2014). Added to this is the growing number of "issue managers" who control information within government agencies. These individuals often field the information requests sent out by access coordinators and decide how to handle them. Because their job is to protect their employer, they deploy strategies to hide and manipulate information to limit government exposure.

In addition to these challenges, there has been a steady decline in compliance with ATI legislation, especially in terms of the amount of information disclosed. Instances where requesters received no information at all increased by nearly 50 percent between 2007 and 2011 (McKie 2012). Other recurrent problems with Canada's ATI regime include:

- *A lack of control over access fees and using fees as a barrier to subvert access.* At the federal level, if the disclosures exceed the five hours of free search time, users are charged for the cost of the disclosure. At provincial and municipal levels in Canada, there is no free search time, meaning fees to access information can be even greater. Moreover, access fees are generally not limited to the actual costs incurred in reproducing and delivering the information.
- *Systemic delays in the release of information.* Canadian ATI laws include loose timelines for responding to requests, and these timelines are routinely violated. Further, there are no consequences for federal agencies that fail to provide the requested information within prescribed timelines.
- *Resource shortfalls.* Some agencies do not devote adequate resources or personnel to fulfilling their duties under the ATIA, and therefore cannot handle the volume of requests they receive.
- *Secrecy provisions.* A number of other Canadian laws override the provisions of the ATIA and are used as a justification to deny information requests or otherwise threaten ATI users. For instance, the *Security of Information Act* makes it illegal for federal government employees in some positions to communicate about their work.

Of course, challenges in accessing information in Canada transcend outdated legislation, lack of resources, and increases in requests. The information landscape has shifted considerably since the implementation of new security protocols following the events of September 11, 2001. Rates of refusal and wait times for access to information in Canada have significantly increased since 2001, and the adequacy or depth of disclosure has declined (Beeby 2013). Not surprisingly, in the post-9/11 period, "security" has become a key justification that is systematically invoked to withhold government information (Nath 2013; Pozen 2005). Added to this, the rise to power of the federal Conservative Party of Canada has resulted in new problems for access and accountability (Gingras 2012). In the run-up to the 2006 federal election, the Conservatives promised to greatly strengthen Canada's access to information laws by providing the federal Information Commissioner with the power to order the release of government information, and to review exclusions made on the basis of cabinet confidentiality. Neither of these proposals ever came to fruition. On the contrary, the Harper government has altered ATI protocols to further restrict public access to information, and Conservative staffers have been found to routinely interfere with ATI processes (Gillis 2014).

The Conservatives often claim that they have responded to more access to information requests during their tenure than all previous governments combined (Bronskill 2014). Although they frame this as evidence of openness and transparency, it reveals a different truth. Citizens typically file information requests as a last resort, when they cannot obtain the information in any other way. Thus, an increase in information requests is not an indicator of transparency. While it may be a sign that more people are becoming aware of access to information protocols, it is also a sign that the government is exercising tight, centralized control over information. The increase in information requests is also the result of several pieces of highly contentious legislation that have been recently passed—most notably the omnibus bills—which have impacted everything from federal sentencing provisions, to Canada's environmental laws, to the governance of the country's Indigenous peoples. This has led opposition parties, journalists, and social activists to rely on access to information laws more frequently in order to make public these kinds of policy decisions and their impacts.

Under the Harper government, scientific and other government research has also been subjected to unprecedented political scrutiny and secrecy provisions. Scientists working for Natural Resources Canada, for example, were informed in 2010 that they would be required to obtain "pre-approval" from the Minister's office before speaking to the media (Gergin 2011). A 2013 survey of federal government scientists commissioned by the Professional Institute of the Public Service of Canada found that 90 percent of them feel they are not allowed to speak freely to the media about their work; a further 86 percent said they would face censure or retaliation for doing so. The Conservatives have even resorted to old-fashioned "book burnings," presumably in an effort to stifle public information and undermine basic research on the environment and climate change (Nikiforuk 2013). In August 2014, it also became known that the government was instructing government employees to delete emails with no so-called "business value" (De Souza 2014), which further opened the door to the destruction of valuable records and documents, including personal correspondence that might otherwise have been available under ATI law. Employees at Environment Canada were even offered an online course operated by the Canada School of Public Service for guidance on what records to delete. In May 2015, the Conservatives pushed through a new omnibus bill containing unprecedented provisions to retroactively alter access to information law and prevent release of any information related to the now defunct long gun registry (Cheadle 2015). Each new scandal provides more evidence that federal organizations are collecting, processing, and storing information as if they were immune from public oversight.

As a result of these challenges, there have been repeated calls for changes to ATI/FOI protocols over the past few years. In April 2013, several Members of Parliament spoke out publicly about how government employees fail to keep adequate records. Elizabeth May of the Green Party, for instance, identified a "Blackberry culture" on

Parliament Hill that scuttles the creation of government records on contentious files (Poynter 2013). Although ATI requests often take months to process, Blackberry instant messages are automatically deleted after 30 days. That same year, Information Commissioner of Canada Suzanne Legault argued that federal budget cuts were hampering the ability of her office to administer the *ATIA* and respond to complaints. The annual report of the Office of the Information Commissioner of Canada indicated that complaints about the federal ATI regime had increased significantly, while response times varied wildly (Bronskill 2013). It is also worth noting that of the 1,045 complaint investigations completed by the Information Commissioner's office in 2013, 78 percent were found to be valid, meaning that federal departments are not processing requests in compliance with ATI law (Berthiaume 2014).

In March 2014, NDP Member of Parliament Pat Martin put forward a private member's bill calling for revisions to the *ATIA*. The bill called for the Information Commissioner to have order making powers, which would allow that office to compel the release of documents from government agencies (Smith 2014). Also in 2014, a federal advisory panel on open government and democracy pleaded for major revisions to the *ATIA*, as did, once again, the Information Commissioner of Canada (Berthiaume 2014; *Toronto Star* 2014). Describing the Canadian system as "fragile and volatile," Legault pointed to a steady decline in the amount of information released under the *ATIA* over the past fifteen years. Just a few weeks later in July, opposition Members of Parliament critiqued the excessive delays in processing ATI requests (Boutilier 2014). Not only were federal departments failing to meet legislated timelines in the release of information, some institutions—like the RCMP—were even refusing to acknowledge the requests they received. Processing delays and time extensions are more than just an annoyance for ATI users; they often prevent the release of information that is directly relevant to public health and safety. For example, the recent time extensions granted to Transport Canada (unjustified extensions according to the Information Commissioner) have caused delays in the release of information surrounding the Lac-Mégantic rail disaster in Quebec (*Globe and Mail* 2014).

It is not only the federal government that is struggling with poor performance on access to information. In September 2014, the British Columbia Information and Privacy Commissioner Elizabeth Denham published a report on the systematic failings of the FOI regime in that province (Newswire 2014). Six months earlier, the provincial government in Alberta was accused of deliberately interfering with FOI requests (Wittmeier 2014). Indeed, the annual FOI audits conducted by *Newspapers Canada* continue to unearth deficiencies in access to information regimes across the country. All of these challenges point to how government agencies manipulate and control information in Canada. Citizens cannot avoid these barriers, but they must be able to recognize and mitigate them in order to effectively use ATI and FOI processes.

Chapter Descriptions

Access to Information and Social Justice brings together a stellar collection of journalists, scholars, and activists who have used ATI/FOI requests in their work. In Chapter 1, professor and journalist Dean Jobb explores strategies for making good use of ATI and FOI laws. Jobb provides readers with practical advice for refining the wording of requests prior to submission, dealing with barriers to access, avoiding delays and high processing fees, submitting follow-up requests, and pursuing appeals. In Chapter 2, esteemed journalist Leslie Young argues that a government's "hidden data" can reveal a great deal about the reasoning behind public policy decisions, how political problems are framed and addressed, and, sometimes, where government policy contradicts its own information. Using an illustrative case study of oil spills in Alberta, Young demonstrates how obtaining these kinds of data can provide citizens with a strong position from which to critique government decision-making.

In Chapter 3, public interest researcher Jeff Monaghan reflects on his extensive ATI research into policing and security initiatives in Canada. Drawing on examples of successful ATI disclosures related to the security-industrial complex, Monaghan critiques current ATI and FOI laws, analyzes the barriers to obtaining information under the *ATIA*, and highlights the need for legal reform. In Chapter 4, Greenpeace's Keith Stewart and Kyla Tanner argue that as the Harper government has increased its support for tar sands expansion, it has systematically closed down opportunities for public debate and public participation in policy-making. To challenge this narrowing of the democratic process, Stewart and Tanner discuss how Greenpeace Canada has used ATI requests as a powerful tool to expose what is going on behind closed doors between the oil-industry lobby and the Harper government.

Drawing on her personal experiences of the federal government's efforts to silence her art exhibits on climate change, in Chapter 5 award-winning author and artist Franke James offers a series of striking examples of how government bureaucrats subvert ATI laws to avoid public accountability. Her focus is on the critical role that citizens and activists can play in challenging information control. In Chapter 6, activist scholars Alex Luscombe and Michael-Anthony Lutfy explain how Canada's federal ATI laws can be used to study the most secretive security intelligence agencies in the country. To highlight the usefulness of ATI legislation and research, the authors examine attempts by state policing agencies to suppress activist activity in Canada, and explore how notions of threat are assembled in intelligence analysis.

In Chapter 7, University of Ottawa professor of criminology Justin Piché reflects on his ATI research regarding prison expansion in Canada. He discusses how he obtained hidden data on the Harper government's prison infrastructure plans, and how he was then able to mobilize and circulate this information to journalists, activists, and public interest researchers. Piché emphasizes the need for effective communication strategies as a way of making the most of ATI disclosures. In Chapter 8, Christopher Parsons, a post-doctoral fellow at the University of Toronto's Citizen Lab and managing director of the Telecom Transparency Project, discusses the methodology and techniques that can be used to learn about state surveillance practices in Canada. He reviews the relative strengths and weaknesses of a number of critical research strategies, including ATI requests, at both the federal and provincial levels. Parsons argues that researchers need to complement the use of ATI requests with other research techniques and adopt a mixed-methods approach to data collection. Finally, our collection closes with a set of short, accessible tips from our authors about how to effectively conduct ATI/FOI requests in Canada.

The successes outlined at the outset of this introduction demonstrate that access to information users can often overcome bureaucratic and political resistance to produce valuable results. A key objective of this volume is to support this work by providing concrete examples of how to navigate ATI/FOI laws, and how to effectively file and broker access to information requests. A second, broader objective is to demonstrate that, in spite of the challenges associated with Canada's current ATI regime, access to information research remains vital for promoting accountability, transparency, and social justice in Canada.

REFERENCES
Ball, D. 2014. Are You Being Monitored? New Tool Helps Find Out. *The Tyee*, April 24.
Beeby, D. 2013. Federal Budget Cuts Undermine Access to Information System. *Vancouver Sun*, April 8.
_____. 2011. Canada Ranks Last in Freedom of Information: Study. *The Globe and Mail*, January 9.
Berthiaume, L. 2014. Watchdog urges 'Change of Culture'. *The Leader-Post*, June 6.
Bishop, C. A. 2012. *Access to Information as a Human Right*. El Paso: LFB Scholarly Publishing.

Boutilier, A. 2014. Federal Data Request Process May Take Months. *Toronto Star*, July 22.

Bronskill, J. 2015. Bring all Branches of Government under Information Law, Watchdog Urges. *Canadian Press*, March 31.

_____. 2014. Federal Advisers Urge Access to Information. *The Canadian Press*, June 18.

_____. 2013. Glitches Mar Access to Information, Official Says. *Toronto Star*, October 18.

Brownlee, J. 2015a. *Academia, Inc.: How Corporatization is Transforming Canadian Universities*. Halifax: Fernwood Publishing.

_____. 2015b. Contract Faculty in Canada: Using Access to Information Requests to Uncover Hidden Academics in Canadian Universities. *Higher Education* (forthcoming).

CBC News. 2011. Public Servants Using Access Laws in Workplace Claims. October 31.

Centre for Law and Democracy. 2013. Global Right to Information Rating. At <rti-rating.org/country_data.php>

Chase, S. 2011. Can Access to Information be Fixed? *The Globe and Mail*, January 15.

Cheadle, Bruce. 2015. Harper Government Retroactively Rewrites Gun Registry Law. *The Canadian Press*, May 13.

Cordis, A. and P. Warren. 2014. Sunshine as Disinfectant: The Effect of State Freedom of Information Act Laws on Public Corruption. *Journal of Public Economics* 115: 18-36.

De Souza, M. 2014. Harper Government asks Public Servants to Delete Emails. *Toronto Star*, August 27.

Fitzpatrick, M. 2012. Oilsands 'Allies' and 'Adversaries' named in Federal Documents. *CBC News*, January 26.

Gergin, M. 2011. Silencing Dissent: The Conservative Record. Ottawa: Canadian Centre for Policy Alternatives.

Gillis, W. 2014. Canadians' Rightful Access to Public Information Being Blocked. *Toronto Star*, April 27.

Gingras, A. M. 2012. Access to Information: An Asset for Democracy or Ammunition for Political Conflict, or Both? *Canadian Public Administration* 55(2): 221-246.

Globe and Mail. 2014. Justin Trudeau's Openness-By-Default. June 12.

Harris, K. 2014. Mentally Ill Inmates Kept in 'Grossly Inadequate' Conditions. *CBC News*, February 27.

Hildebrandt, A. 2014. Pipeline Rupture Report Raises Questions about TransCanada Inspections. *CBC News*, February 4.

_____. 2013. Pipeline Safety Incident Rate Doubled in Past Decade. *CBC News*, October 28.

Holsen, S. and M. Pasquier. 2011. What's Wrong with this Picture? The Case of Access to Information Requests in Two Continental Federal States—Germany and Switzerland. *Public Policy and Administration* 27(4): 283-302.

Jiwani, F. and T. Krawchenko. 2014. Public Policy, Access to Government, and Qualitative Research Practices: Conducting Research within a Culture of Information Control. *Canadian Public Policy* 40(1): 57-66.

Luscombe, A. and K. Walby. 2014. Occupy Ottawa and Conservation Officer Policing. *Canadian Journal of Criminology and Criminal Justice* 56(3): 295-322.

McKie, D. 2012. Access to Information Act Turns 30 Amid Calls for Reform. *CBC News*, July 7.

Millar, M. 2013. Harper Government's Extensive Spying on Anti-Oilsands Groups Revealed in FOIs. *Vancouver Observer*, November 19.

Monaghan, J. and K. Walby. 2012. Making up 'Terror Identities': Security Intelligence and Canada's Integrated Threat Assessment Centre. *Policing and Society* 22(2): 133-151.

Nath, A. 2013. Beyond the Public Eye: On FOIA Documents and the Visual Politics of Redaction. *Cultural Studies – Critical Methodologies* 14(1): 21-28.

Newswire. 2014. Report Reveals Canadian Province is Failing to Meet Access to Information Requirements. September 29.

Nikiforuk, A. 2013. What's Driving Chaotic Dismantling of Canada's Science Libraries? *The Tyee*, December 23.

Ontario Confederation of University Faculty Associations. 2004. Restricted Entry: Access to Information at Ontario Universities. *OCUFA Research Report* 5(4).

Pike, G. 2005. Legal Issues: Freedom of information? *Information Today* 22(4): 17-24.

Poynter, B. 2013. Chilly White North? Canadian Government Secrecy on the Rise. *Christian Science Monitor*, April 5.

Pozen, D. 2005. The Mosaic Theory, National Security, and the Freedom of Information Act. *Yale Law Journal* 115(3): 628-679.

Professional Institute of the Public Service of Canada. 2013. The Big Chill: Silencing Public Interest Science, A Survey. At <pipsc.ca/portal/page/portal/website/issues/science/pdfs/bigchill.en.pdf>

Roberts, A. 2012. WikiLeaks: the Illusion of Transparency. *International Review of Administrative Sciences* 78(1): 116-133.

Savage, A. and R. Hyde. 2014. Using Freedom of Information Requests to Facilitate Research. *International Journal of Social Research Methodology* 17(3): 303-317.

Smith, P. 2014. Information Act 'Terribly Outdated' NDP MP Says. *Ottawa Citizen*, March 19.

Suthar, S. K. 2011. Protecting Freedoms, Guaranteeing Rights: Study of Freedom of Information Act, US and Right to Information Act, India. At <ssrn.com/abstract=2261057>

Toronto Star. 2014. Revamp Access to Information Law, Say Federal Advisory Panel Members. June 18.

Tromp, S. 2010. Notable Canadian News Stories Based on ATIA Requests. At <www3.telus.net/index100/atiastories1>

_____. 2008. *Fallen Behind: Canada's Access to Information Act in the World Context*. At <www3.telus.net/index100/report>

Weber, B. 2013. Study Finds Little Environmental Enforcement in Oilsands Infractions. *The Canadian Press*, July 23.

Wittmeier, B. 2014. Interference Accusations to be Probed. *Calgary Herald*, May 31.

Worthy, B. 2013. Some are More Open than Others: Comparing the Impact of the Freedom of Information Act 2000 on Local and Central Government in the UK. *Journal of Comparative Policy Analysis: Research and Practice* 15(5): 395-414.

CHAPTER I

SEEKING TRUTH FROM POWER: STRATEGIES FOR USING ACCESS LAWS

Dean Jobb

Politicians and bureaucrats love to keep secrets, and it is no secret that using access laws to pry public records from their grasp can be a frustrating, time-consuming process. Access laws and procedures can be complex. Disclosure rules and practices vary by province. It can take months—and in extreme cases, years—for applicants to receive any records. Fee estimates reaching into the thousands of dollars may be levied to cover research and reproduction costs, putting access out of reach for many citizens and researchers. Moreover, a surprising number of government and publicly funded agencies do not have a legal duty to disclose records—an estimated 100 at the federal level alone. And when access laws do apply, some classifications of records are exempt from disclosure, or government officials err on the side of caution and withhold or censor documents that should be made public.

That is the bad news for truth and democracy. The good news is that Canada's access laws, despite these shortcomings, remain a powerful tool for keeping governments somewhat open, honest, and accountable. According to the Supreme Court of Canada: "The overarching purpose of access to information legislation is to facilitate democracy ... It helps to ensure first, that citizens have the information required to participate meaningfully in the democratic process, and secondly, that politicians and bureaucrats remain accountable to the citizenry" (*Dagg v. Canada [Minister of Finance]*

1997). Access laws, note the authors of *Digging Deeper* (2005), a Canadian public records research guide, "offer journalists, researchers and any Canadian citizen the ability to look beyond the public record to learn more about hidden government actions, policies, and decisions" (Cribb et al. 2015: 238). Stanley Tromp (2010), a journalist and access advocate, has identified more than 100 major news stories, published between 2006 and 2010, which relied on Canadian government records obtained using the federal *Access to Information Act*. The subjects ranged from exposés of government stonewalling and waste to investigations of threats to health, safety, the environment, and national security. These stories, Tromp concludes, demonstrate that journalists and others can overcome bureaucratic and political resistance and legislative deficiencies to produce valuable results.

Access laws work to ensure that the public's business becomes a matter of public record. The strategies and advice that follow will help demystify the application process, suggest ways to avoid high fees and long delays, and aid journalists, researchers, academics, and concerned citizens to make the most of their access rights.

Before You File

Do Your Homework: First, make sure an information request is necessary. Many government records are available online, at public libraries, or through informal requests. Departments and agencies issue detailed annual reports of their activities; orders-in-council (decisions and directives of federal and provincial cabinets) are open to public scrutiny; lobbyists must disclose their activities and political parties must reveal who supports them with donations. In most jurisdictions, expenses of elected officials and cabinet ministers, the amounts paid to contractors and suppliers, and the assets of politicians are routinely published or made available at government offices. The federal government also provides an online resource, *Proactive Disclosure*, with links to contracts, grants, travel expenses, and other information that federal departments and agencies make public on an ongoing basis.

Next, verify which public body—and which level of government—holds the records you are seeking. Canada has a patchwork of access laws. The *Access to Information Act* covers the federal government, and each province and the three northern territories have similar legislation. Provincial governments have also introduced laws to make the records of cities, towns, and other local governments subject to access requests. Health Canada, for instance, deals with national health issues that are distinct from the front-line medical services that fall under provincial jurisdiction. It is also important to note that the scope of access legislation varies from province to province. Hospitals, school boards, colleges, and universities are required to disclose records in some but not others. And one province, British Columbia, allows access requests for the records of self-governing societies that regulate professionals, such as lawyers and doctors.

The online publication *Info Source* offers a guide to federal government records that are accessible using the *Access to Information Act* (Government of Canada 2015). The federal government also offers an online resource, the *Access to Information Manual*, which is designed for use by federal employees and provides insights into the scope of the legislation and how it is administered and interpreted. The Canadian Legal Information Institute website offers a searchable database that includes federal, provincial, and territorial access legislation. Use it to determine which law applies to your request and whether the public body is under a legal obligation to disclose records.

Every government department and public agency has a small staff or contact person responsible for processing access requests and assisting applicants. A phone call or email inquiry may be all that is needed to confirm that your application is headed to the correct office. Websites and online staff directories make it easy to track down their contact information. It is often helpful to contact these officials to discuss your proposed request—they have a duty, in most jurisdictions, to guide applicants through the process. They can also suggest ways to refine the scope or wording of a request to avoid delays and excessive search fees. You may even discover that the information is available without making a formal application.

Previous Access Applications: If the information you seek has been released through a previous access request, it should be available almost immediately and at little or no cost. If you know of such a request—either through your research or a news report—contact the government agency involved. It should not be necessary to file another formal request. CBC investigative journalist David McKie maintains the Coordination of Access to Information Requests System (CAIRS) database (2015), a compilation of requests processed under the federal *Access to Information Act*. This is a valuable resource, and not only for determining whether information is already in the public domain. Applicants can see how successful requests were worded and find out more about the types of records available from various agencies.

Preparing the Request

Wording the Request: There is no need to provide a long list of the kinds of records you hope to obtain. An application under the federal act will capture records in all forms, from books and maps to videos and microfilm. Nova Scotia's freedom of information law, for example, defines "record" as including "documents, maps, drawings, photographs, letters, vouchers, papers and any other thing on which information is recorded or stored by graphic, electronic, mechanical or other means." So a simple request for "records" relevant to the application should ensure that nothing is overlooked or excluded. Application forms are available online or from government offices, but in most cases applicants need only submit a letter stating that they are making a request under the access law.

Be Specific: The more specific the request, the faster the response and the less likely the request will be delayed or result in significant search fees. Provide as much information as possible about the records being sought. If you are seeking a specific report, audit, or study, say so. Provide the name of the author, the title, and the approximate date it was completed (if such details are known). If your research suggests the documents were drafted within a certain time-frame, ask only for records created during that period.

Adopt a "Surgical" Approach: When applying for access to an internal report or study that is likely to be lengthy, request access to only the executive summary, table of contents, introduction, and conclusion. The main body of the report or study can be sought later if necessary. Dean Beeby (1997), a journalist with the *Canadian Press* news wire service, recommends an initial request seeking the title page and table of contents of audits and reports, followed by a second round of requests for the full version of those documents that look promising. Applicants seeking databases or other records stored in electronic form can take a similar approach and request access to a database template or sample file. This will confirm the scope of the data, how it is organized, and whether privacy concerns or other barriers will make it difficult to view the entire electronic record.

Another useful approach is to cast a wide net but to narrow the time frame in order to ensure that the number of records subject to the request is manageable. An applicant may seek inspection reports for all bridges within a province or restaurants within a city, for example, but only those completed within the last three months. A request for inspection reports over a period of years is almost certain to become mired in delays given the large volume of records involved, and officials will be justified in demanding hefty search fees. Records often include personal information about individuals who must be consulted before government agencies decide whether to release or withhold the information; if these details are not relevant to your research, consider asking that personal information be excluded from your request to speed up the process.

In short, avoid fishing expeditions. If it becomes clear later that the initial request was too specific and other relevant materials exist, file a follow-up request for additional records.

Broadening the Request: Once you have targeted a specific record, take a step back. Consider broadening your request to include other records created in response to the original. Follow-up reports, briefing notes, and internal correspondence will reveal whether government officials accept or reject the findings of a report or audit and the actions, if any, they plan to take as a result.

Assume the Records Are Available: Do not overthink a request and abandon it because the information you seek might fall within one of the categories exempt from disclosure, such as cabinet secrets, advice shielded by solicitor-client privilege, or confidential information about third parties. The default position under access laws is that all records are accessible. "Exemptions should be exceptional and must be confined to those specifically set out in the statute," one judge noted when called upon to interpret the federal law (*Canada Information Commissioner v. Canada Minister of Employment and Immigration* 1996). Access legislation often allows government officials to use their discretion when deciding whether to rely on an exemption to withhold records, so information that appears to be off-limits may be released. And it is routine for records to be edited to remove material subject to an exemption, allowing the remaining information to be released. The Royal Canadian Mounted Police (RCMP) and other law-enforcement agencies, for instance, are required to release details of the cost of an investigation and other administrative matters, but would be entitled to redact references to suspects and any evidence collected. Many access requests, even those dealing with controversial or sensitive issues, yield more information than applicants expect to receive.

Filing the Request

Enclose the Application Fee: The *Access to Information Act* imposes a $5 application fee, which must accompany the request. Failure to enclose the fee will put the request on hold until payment is received. Application fees vary under provincial and territorial access laws, from $5 to $25. Some jurisdictions allow for online applications, but the requirement that application fees be paid in advance means it is often necessary to submit an application form or letter by mail, accompanied by a cheque to cover the fee.

Request a Fee Waiver or Reduction: Expect additional charges for search time (up to $30 an hour under some access laws) and for assembling and photocopying records. Access officials must provide an estimate of these fees *before* any work is done, allowing applicants to narrow down their request to reduce costs. Applicants also can ask to review the material at the nearest government office to avoid paying for copies of documents of no interest or relevance. The only additional fees will be to reproduce any documents the requester considers important and worth photocopying.

Applicants have the right to ask government agencies to waive or reduce search and photocopying fees. Applicants with modest incomes or working on tight budgets, such as students or researchers from non-profit groups, should request a fee waiver based on financial hardship. Journalists, academics, and others who plan to publish the results of their research can make a strong case that fees should be reduced or waived because the records are matters of public importance and the information will be disseminated to a wide audience. A fee waiver should be requested when the application is submitted and it should also be possible to request a waiver later, after a fee estimate has been provided.

Consider Multiple Requests: Officials who process access requests may have differing opinions on whether an exemption applies to a particular record. If multiple departments or agencies have copies of a record, submit a request to all of them. While it has become common for government officials to coordinate their responses, multiple requests may result in one agency releasing more information than others. And if the request relates to records exchanged with government agencies in the United States or other countries, consider making a parallel request under that country's access legislation, which may provide more generous access than Canadian laws. For instance, a 2011 *National Post* report on Canada's efforts to convince the US government to approve the controversial Keystone XL pipeline was based on records obtained through a US access request (Cribb et al. 2015).

Avoid Privacy Barriers: Information that governments collect and compile about individuals is considered confidential and exempt from disclosure. But this can be an advantage rather than a barrier, since everyone has the right to request access to government records about themselves. For example, the subject of your research may be willing to file a request seeking information about their personal battle with a bureaucracy, and share the information once it is disclosed. In most jurisdictions, application and search fees are not charged to people who apply for personal information in government hands.

Awaiting the Response

Create a File: Keep a copy of the application letter or form and the cheque covering the application fee in case of the unlikely event that your application or payment is lost or misplaced. You should receive a letter from the government agency acknowledging the receipt of your request and stating the deadline for a response. Keep a copy of this and all other correspondence and emails, and make a note of any phone conversations with government officials related to the request. This documentation will be needed if you decide to challenge a decision to withhold records.

Follow Up and Negotiate: Touch base with access coordinators as the deadline approaches for a response to make sure the request is on track. And be prepared to negotiate to reduce fees or to scale back a request that involves more records than expected.

Expect Delays: Most access laws stipulate a 30-day deadline for responding to requests, but governments have the right to extend the time limit if the request involves confidential information or a large number of records. It usually takes more than a month to receive a response, and some applications may be held up for several months or longer. While timely releases of information do occur—particularly when applicants have made requests that are specific and reasonable in their scope—be prepared for the long haul.

Once Records Are Released

Carefully Study the Records Disclosed: Read every document and pore over every word. A single memorandum or email—even a single sentence—may contain enough important information or startling revelations to make the application worthwhile. For example, a Canadian journalist investigating the controversial political deals and lax safety oversight that culminated in the 1992 explosion at Nova Scotia's Westray coal mine, in which 26 miners died, plowed through hundreds of pages of letters, reports, and memos on a multi-million dollar federal loan guarantee to a private firm before finding a key reference to the role the Prime Minister's Office had played in negotiating this financial support. Another reason to read closely is that documents that appear to be duplicates may in fact be earlier drafts that contain additional information. In rare cases, you may even discover that information deleted from one document has been retained in another.

Is Anything Missing? Records and portions of documents that have been withheld should be clearly indicated, along with each exemption the government is relying upon to justify its position that the information cannot be disclosed. Do documents appear to be missing from the paper trail, either because they were overlooked or intentionally withheld? Are there references to actions taken or policies implemented, but no documentation to support these initiatives? Does a report or letter cite additional documents that should have been released? Arrange the records by date to spot any gaps in the chronology that suggest more material should have been released. One journalist seeking information about the RCMP investigation of the Westray mine disaster, for instance, was informed there were no prosecution-related reports on the incident. A later access request, however, yielded a detailed chronology of the prosecution of the mine's managers on charges of manslaughter and criminal negligence, which revealed the existence of several reports that should have been identified and released in response to the initial request (*Nova Scotia, Public Prosecution Service* 1998).

Follow-up Research and Requests: A review of the records released may identify additional relevant documents that did not fall within the scope of your initial request, and these can be sought through a follow-up request. Also, consider a follow-up request for all records created in response to your initial application. Many government agencies single out requests from journalists, advocacy groups, and critics—some federal departments call this practice "amber-lighting" requests—and subject them to additional scrutiny and delay (Roberts 2006). An application for details of how your request was handled could expose such practices. Bear in mind that the records released are only part of the story, or a snapshot. The information obtained will often point your research in new directions, but further inquiries and interviews with key participants are often necessary in order to obtain a more complete picture.

Seek a Second Opinion

Reviews and Appeals: Governments and other public agencies may refuse to release records, but they do not get the last word. Applicants have the right to challenge actions taken in response to their requests, including the exemptions cited to withhold documents, failures to comply with the legislation, and excessive fees. In each jurisdiction, an independent official (e.g., information commissioner, review officer, ombudsman) has been appointed to investigate complaints. These information watchdogs have the power to examine undisclosed records to determine whether government officials have claimed exemptions that are not justified. These reviews may take months to resolve but they cost applicants little or nothing (there is a small application fee in some jurisdictions) and may produce additional records or set important precedents for future research. Even if a review is resolved in the government's favour (refusals to release records are often upheld), applicants will have some assurance that they have been given all of the information they are entitled, by law, to receive.

In five provinces, information commissioners or review officers have the power to order governments to release records if they find there are no grounds for withholding them. Officials in the remaining jurisdictions and the federal information commissioner do not have order powers and can only recommend that information be released. Government agencies sometimes accept these findings and release additional records, but they are under no legal obligation to comply (Roberts 1998).

The struggle may not end there. Applicants in all jurisdictions have the right to appeal to a judge, who has the power to order the release of additional information. The federal information commissioner can go to court on an applicant's behalf if a case could set a precedent for improved access. While court challenges can be expensive and take months to resolve, many applicants have launched appeals that produced additional records and clarified or expanded access laws. One judge, Justice William Kelly of the Nova Scotia Supreme Court, has described access laws as "an important part of the ongoing process of improving the democratic process" (*Atlantic Highways Corporation v. Nova Scotia* 1997) and applicants should, whenever possible, exercise their right to challenge a refusal to release records. Reviews and appeals play a critical role in Canada's access regime.

Go Public: If a government agency has refused to release records that should be open to public scrutiny, or is using delays and search fees to block legitimate requests, the public has a right to know. Journalists often make their access battles public, and other researchers and activists should consider alerting the media when they encounter government stonewalling. Public and media pressure may convince government decision-makers to reduce excessive fees, reverse an overly zealous decision to withhold records, or to accept an information commissioner's recommendations that additional documents should be released.

Exercise Your Access Rights

An access to information request should be considered as part of any investigation into government activities. And the more applications you file, the better you will understand how the legislation works and the more information you will unearth. Despite legal barriers and administrative hurdles, access laws are crucial tools in every researcher's toolkit. Use them.

REFERENCES

Beeby, D. 1997. Address to the Forum of Freedom of Information and Privacy in Nova Scotia. School of Journalism, University of King's College (unpublished).

Coordination of Access to Information Requests System (CAIRS) database. 2015. At <server.carleton.ca/~dmckie/CAIRS/CAIRS.htm>

Cribb, R., D. Jobb, D. McKie and F. Vallance-Jones. 2015. *Digging Deeper: A Canadian Reporter's Research Guide* (3rd edition). Toronto: Oxford University Press.

Government of Canada. 2015. Info Source. At <infosource.gc.ca/index-eng.asp>

Roberts, A. 2006. *Blacked Out: Government Secrecy in the Information Age*. New York: Cambridge University Press.

_____. 1998. Limited Access: Assessing the Health of Canada's Freedom of Information Laws. Freedom of Information Research Project, School of Policy Studies, Queen's University, Kingston, Ontario.

Tromp, S. 2010. Notable Canadian News Stories Based on ATIA Requests. At <www3.telus.net/index100/atiastories1>

LEGAL CASES

Atlantic Highways Corporation v. Nova Scotia, 1997 CanLII 11497 (NSSC).

Canada (Information Commissioner) v. Canada (Minister of Employment and Immigration), 1986 3 FC 63 at para. 69 (TD).

Dagg v. Canada (Minister of Finance), 1997 2 SCR 403 at para. 61.

Nova Scotia (Public Prosecution Service) (Re), 1998 CanLII 3587 (NS FOIPOP).

CHAPTER 2

THE POWER OF NUMBERS:
HOLDING GOVERNMENTS ACCOUNTABLE WITH THEIR OWN DATA

Leslie Young

Governments collect and store a wide range of information on policy decisions, events, and individuals. Some of this information is kept in reports or emails and is accessible through freedom of information (FOI) legislation at the provincial level, and access to information (ATI) legislation at the federal level. Obtaining copies of documents using FOI and ATI requests can be a powerful way to observe the decision-making processes of governments and to hold them accountable for their actions. Governments keep another sort of information, however, which can be just as powerful, if not more so: data. Data is more than just statistical summaries, like those showing that every restaurant in Toronto is inspected at least twice a year (City of Toronto 2012). While useful, this sort of information is readily available on government websites and does not tell you much beyond those numbers. Data is what the government used to create that summary—the records of every restaurant inspection that, when added together, show that health inspectors closed more restaurants in Toronto's Chinatown and Kensington Market than anywhere else (*The Grid* 2012). Data is the raw information. Having this information means that you are free to dig deeper into issues and perform your own analysis. Chances are you might find something more interesting than what is available in the public domain. Of course, data analysis can be a lot of work. It can be boring at times. And it often raises more questions than it answers. So, why spend a week giving yourself eyestrain gawking at a spreadsheet? Because data is extremely powerful.

First, it is a great way to demand accountability. Like other research you undertake through FOI and ATI, you are getting the government's own information. Since they created it, they have a responsibility to explain it. If you have government files showing that ten people died in a provincial jail, you had better believe they will respond. Data also lends you credibility. It allows you to quantify an issue, and to measure it. While an interview with an individual who has been forced to boil her water for months to make it drinkable is compelling, your story is that much more powerful if you can prove that this problem disproportionately affects First Nations communities, as one *Global News* story recently did. Data obtained through ATI showed that one in every five First Nations communities was under a boil-water advisory in 2011, and that one such advisory had been in place for ten years (*Global News* 2012). Where you once had an anecdote, now you have a demonstrable pattern. Data reveals patterns and connections that you might otherwise not have noticed. It can show that water main breaks are clustered in Toronto's suburbs, or that humpback whales are making a comeback off the coast of British Columbia. Finally, data allows you to creatively tell the story—through maps, graphs, or other visual elements—in a way that can help people better understand the issues.

Data Analysis in Practice: The Case of Alberta Oil Spills

When a huge oil spill threatened the water supply of the town of Red Deer, Alberta, in the summer of 2012, many Canadian news organizations covered the story. It was potentially very dangerous to people nearby, and upsetting to residents who saw black crude oil turning their river into a swamp. For its part, the provincial government was concerned about the incident, but reported an encouraging statistic: there are just 1.5 oil spills per 1,000 kilometres of pipeline, a figure that has been steadily dropping over the past few years. The statistic may sound positive, but it leaves out a lot of information. While the oil spill was being contained, CBC Radio did an interview with someone considered to be an expert on oil spills. During the interview, the man casually mentioned that oil spills "happen all the time."

This piqued my interest as a reporter. Was that true? Did oil spills really "happen all the time"? There had certainly been several major spills over the past year alone. So, I set about finding out just how many oil spills there were. It seemed clear that the Alberta government would be involved in oil spills somehow. Perhaps the environment ministry would send cleanup crews to the sites. Or maybe oil companies would call in to report the incidents. I spent a lot of time examining the websites of the provincial environment ministry and energy regulator to find out how oil spills are reported, how they are tracked and monitored, and how they are cleaned up. Calls to the relevant ministries helped to clarify. Then, I filed an FOI request to the Ministry of Environment and Sustainable Development asking for the records of all oil spills, including location, amount spilled, and the company responsible.

Unfortunately, the response was less than stellar—boxes and boxes of paper, rather than the spreadsheet file that was requested. Not only that, but the files were missing essential information, such as records of all major spills that had been reported in the news over the past few years. So, I filed another request to the Energy Resources Conservation Board (now the Alberta Energy Regulator). Eventually, they told me that the records were available for purchase. So I bought them. Inside the Excel file was fairly complete information on over 60,000 incidents since 1975 where crude oil or other chemicals were released. It showed when and where these spills happened. It showed the worst offenders. And it showed that on average, there have been two pipeline spills *every day* in Alberta since 1975.

Figure 2.1: Excel Sheet Showing Alberta Oil Spills

IncidentDate	IncidentNotificationDate	IncidentCompleteDate	Source
01/01/2003 0:00	01/01/2003 0:00	1/24/2003 0:00	Crude Oil Group Battery
01/01/2003 0:00	01/01/2003 0:00	01/01/2003 0:00	Miscellaneous
01/01/2003 0:00	01/01/2003 0:00	1/14/2003 0:00	Oil/Bitumen Satellite
01/02/2003 0:00	01/02/2003 0:00	01/02/2003 0:00	Crude Oil Group Battery
01/02/2003 0:00	01/02/2003 0:00	01/02/2003 0:00	Oil Well
01/03/2003 0:00	01/03/2003 0:00	01/03/2003 0:00	Crude Oil Group Battery
01/03/2003 0:00	01/03/2003 0:00	01/03/2003 0:00	Service Well
01/03/2003 0:00	01/03/2003 0:00	01/04/2003 0:00	Natural Gas Pipeline
01/03/2003 0:00	01/03/2003 0:00	01/03/2003 0:00	Oil Well
01/04/2003 0:00	01/04/2003 0:00	01/09/2003 0:00	Multiphase Pipeline
01/04/2003 0:00	01/04/2003 0:00	01/06/2003 0:00	Multiphase Pipeline
01/04/2003 0:00	01/04/2003 0:00	01/06/2003 0:00	Oil Well
01/04/2003 0:00	01/04/2003 0:00	01/08/2003 0:00	Crude Oil Pipeline
01/04/2003 0:00	3/25/2003 0:00	09/07/2004 0:00	Compressor Station
01/05/2003 0:00	01/05/2003 0:00	01/06/2003 0:00	Oil Sands Plant
01/06/2003 0:00	01/06/2003 0:00	01/06/2003 0:00	Crude Oil Group Battery

By mapping the spill locations, I found one couple who had an oil spill on their farm every year. Showing that map as part of my report reinforced just how many oil spills there actually are, and it allowed people to look up spills affecting their local communities (*Global News* 2013). None of this information was publicly known. Revealing it added important context to the ongoing debate over new and proposed pipeline projects in Canada. It pointed to shortcomings with the province's regulatory and reporting systems. It also led the provincial government to become more transparent about reporting oil spills on its website. You can now go online and download a spreadsheet of recent oil spills. While it remains incomplete, the spreadsheet shows far more information than was disclosed in the past, and the breadth of this information is more revealing than the "1.5 incidents per 1000 km of pipeline" figure that was cited so often by the province.

Strategies for Finding and Accessing Government Data

The story mentioned above could not have been written without data. Without an individual record of each spill, reporters would have to rely on official government statistics. But how do you know whether data on a given topic exists? Part of the answer to this question is common sense: does it seem like something that governments would keep a record of? But there are other questions that can help guide your search. If the answer to any of the following questions is "yes," then it is likely that data exists on your topic.

1. Is this a recurring event?

    If it is the kind of thing that happens regularly, there is a good chance that information is entered into a standardized database.

2. Is money involved? Is there a fine or a fee?

    Generally, governments keep fairly detailed records of financial matters.

3. Were the police involved?

    Crimes, vehicle accidents, and other such matters are well documented by police.

4. Does it require a licence or a permit?

    Businesses and individuals have to apply for licences, and these licences and associated information will be available in a database.

5. Are there inspections?

    Generally, government inspectors must follow a detailed checklist, and their notes (and whether the individual/business passed or failed) are often entered into a database.

6. Is there a reporting requirement; that is, does a company or individual have to report an incident according to the law?

    If so, that information might be entered into a database.

7. Could the incident pose a danger to public health or well-being?

    Governments are fairly good at determining whether something, if unchecked, could pose a danger to the public, and they usually document these things. Whether they act on the information is another matter.

Take the example of a car accident. It fits many of these criteria. Car accidents happen all the time. Serious accidents must be reported and the police are involved. They note various details at the scene, such as the location, contributing factors, and the date and time. Both drivers should be licensed, so their licensing information exists somewhere. The vehicles might have been inspected. And, car accidents are dangerous events, so the government has an interest in tracking them. An FOI request to either the police or provincial department of transportation could yield the date an accident occurred, the number of vehicles involved, contributing factors such as whether one of the drivers was impaired or on their cell phone, and the location of the accident. But how would you get this information? It is simple—you ask for it. First, figure out who is likely to hold the information you require. You need to direct your request to the appropriate government department; otherwise you can end up wasting a lot of time. Guessing wrong is more common than you might think! Try to be certain before you send your request. In general, governments do not freely supply extra information through FOI or ATI. You tend to get exactly what you ask for, no more and no less. This can be particularly true of requests for data. You will only get the bits of information you specifically requested. Other potentially more interesting parts of the database are likely to be left out.

A few basic techniques can help you pinpoint the information you want and properly craft your request. First, learn as much about the database as you can before making your request. A lot of information can be found on government websites. For example, looking up the reporting requirements for an incident can be helpful. They will generally list what information must be reported, so that information is likely in the database. Internet searches can help too. A site-specific search (e.g., "site:forces.gc.ca procurement") can turn up disused web pages that you may not have otherwise found through navigating the main site. For instance, you might find a training manual explaining to government employees how to use a database, including a detailed description of what it contains. This would be a gold mine of information about databases held by the department. By including "site:" before the domain name, you limit results to web pages from that domain only, which ensures that you do not obtain thousands of unrelated results. Also try adding a file type (e.g., "site:forces.gc.ca filetype:xls procurement"). Searching for Excel sheets, comma-separated values (.csv) files, and PDFs can sometimes turn up interesting results. You might find a copy of a useful database hidden somewhere in the back of a website, saving you the trouble of making an information request.

The simplest way to find out what is in a database is to ask. Figure out who maintains the database and send them an email. Ask for a "records layout," which is essentially a list of all the column headings in the database. Then, as you file your request, you can make specific reference to the database's name and contents. For example: *"I request a copy of the Transport Incidents database, including information on the date, type of vehicle, location, and contributing factors."* This same request could be made without naming the database, for example, *"I request a list of all transport incidents, including information on the date, type of vehicle, location, and contributing factors."* Although the latter type of request may work, knowing that a specific database exists can help a great deal if the government claims otherwise or pushes back against the request. Here is an example of an FOI/ATI request for a database (excluding the necessary contact information and not necessarily naming the correct provincial FOI law as the names vary between provinces):

To Whom It May Concern:

This is a request under the Freedom of Information and Protection of Privacy Act.

I request an electronic document showing all reports of bedbugs in the province, including the date of the report, the date inspected, and the first three characters of the postal code (FSA, or forward sortation area) of addresses where bedbugs have been reported. The time frame of this request is for 2014 or the most recent complete year available.

Please provide this information in an electronic database or spreadsheet format, such as Microsoft Excel, .csv, or Microsoft Access.

Sincerely,
Your Name

There are a few important points to reflect on here. This request specifically mentions what information you are looking to obtain, down to what are likely column headings in the database. It specifies a date range. To anticipate privacy objections, it does not ask for the full address of homes that have reported bedbugs. It only asks for the first three characters of the postal code, which in most cities narrows it down to the neighbourhood level. It is much less likely that governments will object to this because you are including hundreds of addresses in the same area. Think about privacy when you make requests. You will probably not get the names or addresses of individuals, but if you can blur someone's identity, you can still argue for and get usable information.

The request also mentions the file format you want—comma-separated values (.csv), an Excel file, or a database such as Microsoft Access. There is a reason for this. The natural preference of most governments is to release information as a flat Adobe PDF file. Some governments even send stacks of physical paper. This is fine for most documents, but it is a real problem when it comes to data. It is hard to analyze a photocopy of an Excel table for patterns, so make sure to ask for a readable data format. And if you are given a PDF, go back to the information coordinator and ask for a better file. It is worth noting that the federal *Access to Information Act*, as well as some provincial legislation, contains provisions for providing information in the format that it is requested:

> The head of a government institution shall, without regard to the identity of a person making a request for access to a record under the control of the institution, make every reasonable effort to assist the person in connection with the request, respond to the request

accurately and completely and, subject to the regulations, provide timely access to the record *in the format requested* (Access to
Information Act—section 2.1, emphasis added).

Start by "asking nicely" for a better file format, as information
coordinators are often happy to provide it. But in the end, you may
have to demand it. Still, a few days of phone calls could save significant time rather than trying to scan, retype, or crack a PDF or
paper file. Finally, if you find that the government agency is being
too restrictive and not giving you the data you require (or withholding crucial information), there are a few options.

First, make sure you file complaints. Information commissioners
at the provincial and federal levels have varying powers to investigate complaints, and in some jurisdictions they can even bring a case
to court on your behalf or issue orders with which the government
must comply. Often just filing the complaint is enough to prompt
a response from a government agency. There are times when it is
easier for them to give you what you want rather than go through a
lengthy complaints process. But sometimes they are stubborn. Even
at the federal level, where the commissioner's powers are limited, it
is still worth filing a complaint. The commissioner's annual report
notes particularly egregious cases and offers some statistics. There
is a small hope that your problems will at least be recorded and perhaps later contribute to changes in the ATI system.

Second, if you are having trouble you can always look elsewhere.
Other countries have FOI and ATI laws too, and depending on what
you are seeking, you might be able to get information from another
country. Many journalists have had success using FOI requests in
the United States to investigate cross-border issues. FOI law in the
US does not require you to be an American citizen to file a request.
And in many cases, they are much more open to releasing information than Canadian governments.

A Note on Open Data

Governments at all levels are increasingly publishing "open data"—data sets freely available for download on their websites. Before you file a formal FOI or ATI request, it is worth checking whether some or all of the information you want is already online. If so, great! Unfortunately, governments tend to choose the least controversial data sets to be part of their open data programs. With the notable exception of Statistics Canada, a lot of what is online is, frankly, boring and largely irrelevant for journalism or activism work—things like the location of water fountains in Calgary's city parks, for example. Often, open data is best used in conjunction with data obtained through FOI or ATI. Obtaining a blank map file from an open data site can help you map and analyze your data. Or, matching income data from Statistics Canada with your data can add a whole new level of analysis. It is worth keeping an eye on open data websites to see what is there, but while they are slowly being improved, open data is unlikely to replace the FOI and ATI process.

Avoiding Errors by "Cleaning" Your Data

Once you have your data, the first step is to take a careful look through it. Is everything you asked for there? Do you understand what all the column headings mean? Are words abbreviated or coded in a way you do not understand? If your database is incomprehensible, you can try asking the information coordinator who provided your data for a handbook, instruction book, or guide to the database. Or, you can send them a list of abbreviated words and ask for a translation. The coordinator is often able to provide this information within a couple of days, though at times they may direct you to a media relations or a communications department.

But let us assume that you have your data and you understand everything that it contains. You might be tempted to start analyzing—don't! Take a step back and review your data. Unfortunately, government data, like all databases, is often full of errors. These might be simple typos, such as "Otawa" instead of "Ottawa." Or the month "September" might appear in your database as "Sept.," "Sept," "Sep," or "september." These misspellings and variations are simply the result of many different people contributing to the database at different times, and making mistakes. However, this can really disrupt your analysis. If you are counting how many car accidents happened in September, but you forget to count all the "Sept." accidents, your final tally will be wrong. So you need to check through your data and try to spot these variations. There are a few shortcuts for this, such as using the "Sort" and "Filter" functions in spreadsheet programs (discussed below), or a computer program such as "Open Refine," but a lot of errors can be spotted simply by knowing your data. Sometimes a number can be typed in wrong too, which is usually an error that is difficult to spot. If something looks or feels wrong to you, it probably is. Make sure you run your data concerns by the relevant government department before publishing. You will want to fix as many errors as possible before you start your analysis. And before you start typing new information into your database, save a copy. You want to keep your original file intact, in case you need to go back to it for some reason.

Analyzing the Information and Spotting the Story

So you have your data, and it has been cleaned up. Now what? Like anything else in journalism or research, you start asking questions. Some good questions to ask about any data set are:

- What is the highest number in your data?
- The lowest?
- The most frequent?
- Does anything stand out?
- Has something increased or decreased over time?

You answer these questions by analyzing the data. One of the best tools for doing this is Microsoft Excel or a similar spreadsheet program. Often the simplest way to identify information is by using the "Sort" function. Sorting just means changing the order of your data—arranging it from smallest to largest, earliest to latest, or alphabetically. This is easy to do in Excel. Simply select a column by clicking just above it, then choose Sort & Filter, then Sort from the menu bar along the top (it is also found under the "Data" tab).

Figure 2.2: Sorting in Excel

Q	R
Source	CauseCategory
Oil Well	Conversion
Natural Gas Pipeline	Equipment Failure
Natural Gas Pipeline	Equipment Failure
Natural Gas Pipeline	Equipment Failure
Crude Oil Group Battery	Conversion
Miscellaneous	Conversion
Natural Gas Pipeline	Conversion
Gas Well	Conversion
Natural Gas Pipeline	Conversion
Oil Well	Conversion
Gas Plnt Acid Gas Flr/Inj	Conversion
Miscellaneous	Conversion
Multiphase Pipeline	Conversion
Multiphase Pipeline	Operator Error
Oil Well	External
Crude Oil Group Battery	Conversion
Miscellaneous	Conversion
Water Pipeline	Conversion
Service Well	Equipment Failure
Gas Well	Equipment Failure
Service Well	Equipment Failure
Natural Gas Pipeline	Equipment Failure

Figure 2.3: Sorting in Excel

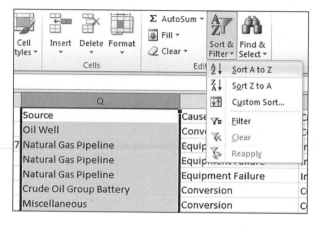

Another useful tool is the "Filter" function. Filtering allows you to display a selection of your data—only incidents that happened in British Columbia, for example. Again, click above the column so that the entire column is highlighted. Then choose Sort & Filter, then Filter.

Figure 2.4: Filtering in Excel

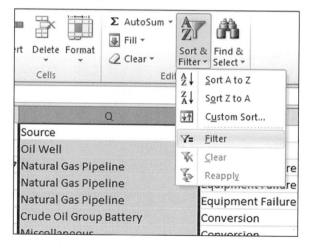

A small arrow will appear at the top of the column. Then, you can select with the checkboxes the data you would like displayed.

Figure 2.5: Filtering in Excel

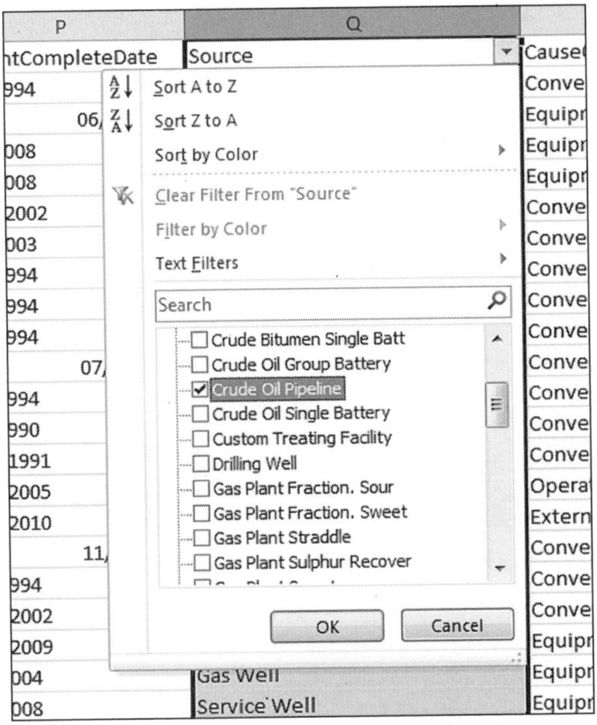

Excel is also good at performing calculations. You can subtract to find the difference between two columns, calculate percentages and percentage change, find an average, count the number of incidents that fit certain criteria, and so on. Most data analysis requires little more than simple arithmetic. There is a lot more you can do, and there are many tutorials and even classes available online that can help. One particularly good resource is Datadrivenjournalism.net.

Keep in mind what you are looking for as you do your analysis. Try to spot outliers and identify trends. And as you question your data, does it prompt any questions in return? For example, does it make you want to know:

- Why did something increase so quickly?
- Why is there so much more in this neighbourhood as opposed to that one?
- Why do so many events happen in the summer?

This is the fun part of the analysis. Once you have identified something interesting in your data, you need to find out why it is the way it is. If whatever you found seems illogical and wrong, it could just be a mistake in the data itself, or perhaps in your calculations. So check with others.

Experts in the field, whether they are scientists, lawyers, academics, economists, or non-governmental organizations, can be a good resource. Presenting them with a summary of your findings can be a great way to get insight on the topic. You may also want to borrow a trick from journalists: find real people. If you can find someone who was affected by the kind of incident you are looking at, or someone who actually shows up in your data, you will gain valuable insight and credibility, as well as an interesting personal story to tell. For example, in a *Global News* series examining the practice of immigration detention, finding an individual who was actually being held in prison for violating immigration laws made a huge difference (*Global News* 2014a). By having him tell his story about why he fled Iran, why he is afraid to go back, and how Canadian immigration authorities have treated him, the story exposed how immigration detention affects ordinary people who are in an extremely vulnerable position.

If you are looking at particular events, you might be able to find a compelling example in your data and find more information about it. Describing an event as it unfolded, step-by-step, can also be a good way to tell a story and get people interested in your issue. This was done to great effect by the *Toronto Star* recently in a story about airplane near misses on runways. The author introduced the story by describing a plane landing at Toronto's Pearson

International Airport, when an air traffic controller realized that there was something on the runway:

> The controller issued urgent orders to the Air Canada crew to abort their landing to avoid the mystery target—instructions that were ignored. On the radar screen, the two targets merged—a nightmare scenario for any air traffic controller. The Air Canada aircraft touched down safely, its crew oblivious to their near-brush—their flight had passed less than 50 feet over a van that had driven into their path (*Toronto Star* 2013).

Leaving your story or research at the data analysis stage is, generally, to leave it incomplete. Not only is it more interesting for people to read about if you have storytelling elements, with data alone you will be presenting a finding without explaining why it is happening, why we should care, or how the problem might be addressed.

Think about how you want to present your story. A data-based story lends itself to creative presentation methods, such as maps or graphs. The key is simplicity. Make sure that your graphic demonstrates one idea—for example, that the number of overcrowded prisons has grown. Cramming too many ideas into a single graphic makes it more difficult for readers to understand. Google Maps is a good start for mapping projects, and Datawrapper is a good choice for simple line and bar graphs. Both are free to use and relatively easy to learn.

Accountability: Bringing Your Findings to the Authorities

Accountability is where a data story can really shine. At this point, you have obtained government data. You have analyzed it and found something interesting—a pattern, an unusual event, or a shocking set of numbers. You have talked to experts in the field and people affected by the issue you are researching. Now, you need to talk to the government.

You might be tempted to publish without talking to the authorities, maybe to surprise them, maybe to keep your story secret until publication. That is fine while you are working on the story, but you should not publish without first giving the government or other parties (upon whom your story might reflect negatively) a chance to respond to your findings. There are several reasons for this. First, if you are a journalist, it is a basic principle of journalistic ethics (and legal importance) to give affected parties a chance to respond. You would not publish a story where someone is accused by a co-worker of embezzlement without allowing them a chance to comment on the allegations. A data story is no different—only that the individual or organization might have to more thoroughly refute any allegations of wrongdoing, since you have documentary proof. You should also provide the affected party with your full conclusions and how you arrived at them so they have all the information they need to respond intelligently.

Even if you are not a journalist and do not feel bound by these ethical considerations (though you should check libel laws to make sure you are in the clear to write your report without consultation), you should still consider taking your story to the database holder before publication. One good reason is to avoid embarrassment. It is entirely possible that the data was incomplete, that you made an error in your calculations, or that there is a more benign explanation for what you are seeing. You may not find this out unless you talk to the people who created the database. If you go ahead and publish, you could be made to look foolish. In fact, if the story is uncontroversial, you should consider mentioning it to the government sooner so they can help you work through the data and keep you from wasting a lot of time on an unimportant issue.

Finally, you should not assume that the government is unaware of your research. They gave you the information in the first place, after all. FOI departments talk to communications departments, and the government will often be well aware of what information is going out, particularly if it is controversial. Some departments, where the law does not prohibit identification of requesters, even have communications or media relations representatives call requesters directly after they submit an information request, to ask if they need help finding anything. So your story is probably not as secret as you think.

Bringing your information to the government does not have to be a chore. Use the opportunity to ask important questions: Why did this happen? Since the government knew about it, why did they allow it to continue? Are there any plans to change the policy? Was the information ever examined? Why not? Since you have documented proof not only of a trend or event, but also that the government was aware of it and recorded it, you can ask strong questions and not accept weak answers. You are in a much more powerful position from which to question authorities than you would be with a handful of examples or personal anecdotes. Use data to get answers, and if the answers are insufficient, say so. Write about it. Get enough people's attention and the government will respond.

Why Data?

Maybe you are feeling a bit exhausted after reading this chapter. Data research through FOI and ATI can be a lot of work: finding the data, writing the request, convincing the database holder to release the information, cleaning the data, analyzing it, and doing extra research to back up your findings. So why bother?

I bother because there is often no other way to get the information. I could have asked the Canada Border Services Agency (CBSA) how many people had died while in immigration custody. They may have told me. They may not have. But by requesting data on detainees through ATI, I forced them to provide me with something. I learned where and when these people died, where they were from, and how long they had been detained. Using these clues, I was able to look for more information from coroners' inquests, news reports, police forces, and correctional institutions. I found other people who were not enumerated in the data, showing that my database was likely incomplete. I was able to identify eleven people whose deaths were linked to immigration detention and write reports on many of them, giving them a name and outlining the circumstances of their deaths. I was also able to bring this information to the CBSA and get them to confirm that yes, these people had died while in immigration detention, and to bring some context to the well-reported suicide of an immigration detainee in Vancouver (*Global News* 2014b). I would not have discovered these people without the data. It provided me with the clues I needed to find out more about the lives of these individuals, and point to shortcomings in the government's approach.

Data will help you identify patterns that you may not otherwise have seen, find out about events that you may not otherwise have heard of, and give you the proof you need to closely question the government on its actions and policies. So is data research worth it? Try it and see.

REFERENCES

City of Toronto. 2012. DineSafe Inspection and Disclosure System. At <toronto.ca/health/dinesafe/system.htm>

Global News. 2014a. 'I'm Not a criminal': Jailed With No Charge, No Sentence, No Oversight. November 5.

_____. 2014b. Deaths in Detention: CBSA's Fatal Failure to Learn from its Mistakes. November 5.

_____. 2013. Crude Awakening: 37 Years of Oil Spills in Alberta. May 22.

_____. 2012. First Nations Enduring Decade-Old Boil Water Advisories. January 20.

The Grid. 2012. Are You Going to Eat That? At <thegridto.com/life/food-drink/toronto-food-safety/>

Toronto Star. 2013. Runway Incursions a Threat to Aviation Safety. May 6.

CHAPTER 3

FOUR BARRIERS TO ACCESS TO INFORMATION:
PERSPECTIVES OF A FREQUENT USER

Jeffrey Monaghan

Canada's *Access to Information Act* (*ATIA*) is a legal framework that allows government records to become declassified through requests for information stored within government departments. The *ATIA* has many deficiencies, but for social justice researchers it presents a useful tool for accessing the "live archive" of government practices (Walby and Larsen 2012). The usefulness of the *ATIA* as a research tool has been transformed, in large part, through the digitalization of governance. New government information storing networks combined with the regular use of computerized technologies have resulted in a copious volume of records. These technology practices mean that documents are more readily available—at least on the plain of search, discovery, and retrieval. Whereas previous practices of data management involved nearly ungovernable and prolific spaces of filing cabinets, and boxes upon boxes of archived files, today's information management tools rely on networks, hard drives, and emails. This renders the vast enterprise of government more accessible, at least in theory.

As a frequent user of the *ATIA*, I engage with practices of information access while remaining conscious of their limits. Over the past decade, I have logged over 330 ATI requests, most of which have been at the federal level. As an academic working from a critical perspective on issues of security, policing, and social control, many of my ATI requests involve looking at sensitive topics and secret materials. I have nonetheless used the *ATIA* to gather large volumes of records on these kinds of issues. My purpose here is to reflect on some of my ATI research by describing four major barriers to using the *ATIA*: 1) the political control of information; 2) fees and time delays; 3) document retrieval inconsistencies; and 4) the discretionary nature of redaction practices. I outline these barriers to further our understanding of the ATI process and to help ATI users to develop counter strategies. Researchers need to understand the mechanics and deficiencies of the system in order to better strategize ways to access information.

Although I focus on the limitations of the *ATIA*, I would like to stress the importance of ATI frameworks for keeping watch over the activities of governments. The use of ATI is unique because it provides unparalleled access to the "backstage" of government operations. Unlike textual records from public sources, documents obtained by means of ATI requests are often "working documents": when left unredacted, they are records that reveal the establishment of programs, the formulation of decisions and strategies, and the communications between workers tasked with programming and implementation. *ATIA*-generated records also raise important questions about the availability of more detailed records that may be accessed by researchers at a later date.

As it stands, however, the *ATIA* remains a terrain of visibility more akin to reading a text through a keyhole than under a microscope. While some of the failures of ATI-based research are specific to poor performance within ATI offices, much of the frustration stems from systematic deficiencies that are the product of an antiquated statutory framework. While this chapter does not offer any prescriptions for changing the legal framework of ATI, knowing how to navigate and negotiate the roadblocks that arise when seeking sensitive documents is critical for helping researchers to overcome many of the pitfalls of ATI investigations.

Political Control of Information

Access to information and freedom of information legislation operate on the assumption that individuals can request information from
the state, and that state authorities will act in an impartial manner
to pass along requested information. The system is built upon trust,
even more so because requested information usually deals with issues
that have not yet been publicized. Allegations that "political" considerations or influence have impacted the *ATIA* process strike at the
very legitimacy of the ATI system.

There are a number of ways we can interpret political interference. First, and most acknowledged, is the direct involvement of political partisans in the *ATIA* process. Less acknowledged, but arguably
more insidious, are institutional mechanisms (structural policy-prac-
tices) that guide or direct ATI information flows. Finally, there is a
more informal process of political intervention, where "political" is
understood in a broader sense of ATI offices working to support the
norms of their institutions.

A number of texts have documented formal processes of political interference. Canada's Office of the Information Commissioner
(OIC) has investigated some of these claims, most notably the case of
political staffer Sebastien Togneri who was involved with ATI interference at Public Works (OIC 2010). In 2013-14, the OIC was actively
investigating delay and interference within eight different government agencies (OIC 2014). Other studies have examined a government process known as "amber-lighting" or "red-flagging," which
involves opening up a direct line of communication between ATI offices and ministerial offices in regard to potentially contentious files
(Hameed and Monaghan 2012; Rees 2003; 2012). As a "political
surveillance process," Rees (2012: 31) argues that amber-lighting
is a sophisticated, government-wide practice where documents are
not released to the requester "until after copies of the records [have]
been sent to the government's spin doctors." Amber-lighting allows

political and communications officials "to view sensitive records, to question access and FOI staff about what they intend to release, and to delay release until they are satisfied that they have identified all troublesome issues and prepared their political masters with a soothing public response" (Rees 2003: A.32).

Government sources prefer to describe amber-lighting as a consultation process, rather than interference. According to an email from Citizenship and Immigration Canada access coordinator Heather Primeau, the government is "amber-lighting" access requests that are considered to be politically sensitive (Thompson 2006). In the email she clearly defines the purpose of amber-lighting when she writes, "the amber-light process is a heads up process to advise senior management of upcoming access to information releases that may attract media or political attention." While amber-lighting has received some public scrutiny, these practices have continued and even accelerated under new measures of information and communications control. As I detail below when discussing complaints mechanisms, overt political interference is difficult to investigate and the OIC has been unable to rectify these problems.

While amber-lighting is a formalized process that allows political staff to become directly involved in the release of ATI documents, there are other policy developments that allow for more nuanced political interference. For example, recent changes to cabinet confidence protocols have altered the process of making redactions to contentious files subject to potential cabinet deliberation. A cabinet confidence is loosely defined as something that has been prepared for (or seen by) the federal cabinet. Under Section 69 of the *ATIA*, officials can withhold records that are (or have been) reviewed by the cabinet. Once a confidence designation has been invoked, the records remain sealed off from public scrutiny for 20 years. In July 2013, the Treasury Board—the government department responsible for the administration of the *ATIA*—issued a non-publicized directive that transformed the cabinet confidence designation. The directive transferred the responsibility for determining whether information is excluded as a cabinet confidence from the Privy Council Office (PCO) to Department of Justice Canada lawyers. According to the Treasury Board, this reform was meant to improve the timeliness of responses since PCO consultations are often onerous. In critiquing the move, however, the OIC (2014: 20) stated that there is a "real possibility that the application of Section 69 will vary from institution to institution and that the Commissioner's investigative process will be complicated by a lack of standardization." Early indications suggest that the policy has indeed resulted in broader exemptions (Brewster 2014). Moreover, complaints to the OIC regarding Section 69 redactions have increased dramatically: by 65 percent between 2012-13 and 2013-14 alone.

As these recent reforms to cabinet confidence processes suggest, a lack of central enforcement of ATI principles results in departments implementing distinct processes to address information release. This is especially true when it comes to sensitive information. Based on annual evaluations from the OIC, the Department of National Defence (DND) regularly ranks as one of the most opaque departments and, in recent years, it has altered its policy instruments to block information that could be politically volatile. One episode that was made public relates to the DND's response to an ATI request that formed the basis of a news report during an election. The disclosure detailed lapsing procurement spending due to mismanagement—a topic that always creates news coverage—and the information reflected poorly on the Conservative Party, which campaigned on providing the military with additional equipment (Pugliese 2012).

In response to the news that damaged the Conservative government's public messaging, Vice-Admiral Bruce Donaldson (vice chief of defence staff) issued a CANFORGEN directive instructing DND employees to be highly biased toward protecting potentially sensitive information. The directive stated: "Information that is not sensitive to the national interest, and therefore not classified, should also be examined to see if it is *sensitive to other than the national interest*, and therefore requires an appropriate designation of either Protected A, B, or C" (Pugliese 2012, emphasis added). While the military likes to keep a distance from explicit political partisanship, there is a strong affinity within the military establishment for a policy of increased defence spending. The CANFORGEN directive can be read as an attempt to protect the military's current political bosses by up-classifying materials that are sensitive to "other than the national interest," which is little more than an esoteric way of saying Conservative political interests.

Finally, it is important to underline how ATI work (like most other work) takes place within certain normative environments, where workers "perform" according to the norms and values of their institutions. As outsider researchers, we should be conscious that ATI offices exist within a broader institutional context that complicates the "independence" of the ATI process. ATI workers who act as representatives of *ATIA* users in particular departments are, first and foremost, employees of those departments. When "tasking" project areas to turn over requested materials, these officers must balance requester demands within their broader normative environments. Often program areas (offices of primary interest) will feel intruded upon when tasked with information requests. Many of these program areas are overworked. If unsatisfied with document production, ATI staff have a difficult task of balancing their statutory duties to assist requesters and their desire to avoid becoming a burden on their co-workers. ATI officers and document-holders share the same workplace, they are likely to work together on future files, and they share many of the same interests, class privileges, and sports pools. Moreover, ATI officers are more likely to want to satisfy their departmental bosses than an ATI user.

It is easy to see how these workplace dynamics can result in ATI officers being "caught in the middle" (or at least perceiving that they are) between workplace allegiances and statutory requirements to assist "outsiders" (i.e., ATI users). As an example, I will paraphrase a conversation on a file regarding a UN meeting in New York attended by high-ranking Canadian officials on the issue of sharing "best practices" related to the surveillance of "homegrown extremism." My ATI request targeted specific documents, from specific meetings, on a specific day, at a specific time, attended by specific individuals. The ATI officer, Linda Polowin, phoned to inform me that the department—the Department of Foreign Affairs and International Trade (DFAIT)—was unable to locate the records. I suggested that outcome was difficult to accept given the specificity of the request. Polowin replied: "Are you a student? You need to understand that government is big. This is a really big department." After being pressed about the specificity of the request, Polowin conceded that the claims of non-existent records were unfounded and that the office of primary interest (OPI) was simply not turning over documents. Part of the difficulty centred on one of the individuals—a high-placed manager—who attended the meetings being on leave, and the current staff being unable to locate the records. It was clear that Polowin had limited powers of persuasion, or was not interested in pursuing the matter.

On October 4, 2013, Polowin sent me a two-page release—with both pages redacted. Surprised by the low quantity of documents, I emailed to inquire whether she believed a thorough search for the records had been conducted. Polowin replied:

> As specified in my cover letter to you, where the following wording was included: Foreign Affairs, Trade and Development Canada's involvement was limited arranging the meetings on the enclosed agenda and accompanying Ms. Galadza [Public Safety Canada] to the meetings. No other background material was *prepared* by this department (emphasis added).

By focusing on the *preparation* of the document—despite my request specifying *in the possession of* the department—Polowin unilaterally limited the scope of the request. She concluded: "In answer to your question. Yes, I am confident that the program area who responded to this request did provide any and all records that this institution is *in possession of*" (emphasis added). An important element of this response demonstrates how an ATI officer can re-scope (despite her inconsistencies in the letter) to give a rationale for limiting the disclosure of records. For whatever reason, the OPI did not want to gather or release the information, and Polowin rationalized the non-compliance of her peers with a unilateral re-scoping and a strong defence of the OPI's turnover of documents. I came to the conclusion that Polowin was likely complicit in quashing an information request in order to protect her peers because the same (simultaneous) request with Public Safety Canada turned over 220 pages, many of which were both produced by and in the possession of DFAIT.

It is true that the government is "big." The volume of textual records produced by governments can be overwhelming. Yet, ATI offices regularly respond to requests with letters indicating that "no records exist," even in cases where documents clearly do exist. It is a simultaneously comical and frustrating process for ATI users. Without an institutional arrangement that integrates elements of independence between ATI officers and document-holders, political interference as a normative practice is as natural as Dr. Frankenstein's monster.

Time Delays and Fees

Excessive time delays and fees represent the most immediate barrier for ATI users. Regulations around fees and delays are detailed in the *ATIA*. Paragraph 9(1)(b) of the *Act* allows institutions to extend the due date for a request for a "reasonable" period of time when consultations with other institutions are necessary but cannot be completed within the original 30-day time limit. Treasury Board of Canada Secretariat policy requires that extensions be as short as possible. Under paragraph 11(2) of the *Act* and in accordance with Access to Information Regulations, institutions are allowed to charge search fees of $10 for each hour in excess of a requester's first five hours. The charging of fees is currently under dispute because of language in the *ATIA* regulations, which states that institutions can only charge fees for searches of "non-computerized" records.

Central to this dispute is what constitutes "computerized" and "non-computerized" records. For example, in a recent request I asked for a word search of the National Security Criminal Investigations Suspicious Incident Report database that is managed by the RCMP. The RCMP responded that each incident report is taken from the web platform and rendered into a separate PDF file, then filed (hard copy) within a particular detachment. After a series of emails and an agreement to significantly scale back the time period of the search (three years to one year), the RCMP indicated that the file would require 27 billable hours ($270) in search fees. I replied that I would eliminate the word search by taking all entries for the calendar year (which would increase the workload of the ATI officer in processing, but eliminate the billable component of the search). In a comical illustration of what Didier Fissin (2013) describes as arbitrary bureaucratic practices of "petty exceptionalism," the RCMP sent a new cost estimate that totalled 175+ hours of billable search time for a total fee of $1,700. Despite the request dealing with entries into a new, state-of-the-art digital database, the internal practices of the department render the database virtually inaccessible to ATI users.

A "duty to assist" is spelled out in subsection 4(2.1) of the *Act*, which requires institutions to make every reasonable effort to respond to requests accurately and in a timely fashion. However, ATI users are frequently frustrated by fee requirements and delays. In part, this is a result of the hodgepodge of practices that have developed in departments. Although there are formal requirements for search fees and delays, ATI users will encounter different responses from different departments. For example, when making a request with Indian Affairs, users will almost invariably receive a fee request. But when making a request with the DND, even a very large request, users will rarely be asked for fees (and like DFAIT, search fees for requests to the DND are often waived). One reason why some departments rarely charge fees stems from an unstated and unwritten compromise, where departments that regularly invoke time extensions forgo fee charges on the basis that the request will not be released anywhere close to the 30-day statutory requirement. Departments such as the DND will sometimes "split" complex requests into multiple parts at no charge. While these processes can be helpful and beneficial, this hodgepodge of practices means that ATI users must negotiate access based on internal, informal, and largely unknown departmental procedures, rather than general policies and guidelines at the national level.

A number of OIC investigations underscore the problems associated with fee assessments, and long and unreasonable delays have been a constant point of discussion in OIC reports. In my research, there have been numerous files that have encountered delays and high fee assessments. Though I have (regrettably) not kept track of institutional delays, the dominant response to my requests has included long extensions. On a number of files, these extensions have not been met. The most ludicrous example involves a request I filed on a Canada Border Services Agency (CBSA) contribution to a border enhancement program in Palestine (A-2010-01481). Initiated in July 2010, the request has remained in progress for almost five years. Long past the official extension, ATI officers at CBSA occasionally send me correspondence to see if I am still interested in the file. In May 2014, for example, Tanya Wagdin wrote: "Your Access to Information request from 2010 has been reassigned to me as we have now finally completed the consultation process. As this request is four years old, I wanted to know if you were still interested in receiving these records." In fact, May 2014 was the *second* time Wagdin was assigned to this request and, when asked about timelines in November 2011, she acknowledged that the file was "quite late."

In an email from October 2012, after I submitted a new request for a document that (unbeknownst to me) was included in an earlier request, Wagdin wrote: "There are approximately +800 pages which we are processing for that request. I also believe that the majority of the records may be exempted under sections 13(1) and 15(1) of the *Act*." I was asked to consider "abandoning" the more recent request (which improves the CBSA's statistics) to wait for the initial request. I acquiesced, this time to a new ATI officer, Rita Lattanzi-Thomas, and was informed that "once I receive the consultation responses from the other government departments, I will make your request my top priority." I wrote in January 2013 to Lattanzi-Thomas, then again in February, then I received a response from Acting Team Leader Robert Pupovac, with whom I originally started the file back in 2010. Pupovac informed me that consultations were ongoing, but a separate ATI on a related topic (A-2010-04262) was prepared for release. Upon receiving A-2010-04262 in the following weeks, I asked Pupovac for clarification. The file was heavily redacted and I wanted to know the volume of redactions. A typical practice in other departments is to number the pages of an ATI release. Often, for redacted pages, there will be break pages that say something like "Pages 100-110 are redacted according to Sections A, B and C." The CBSA release, which totalled only 55 pages, contained no page numbers or redaction information. In response to my email, Pupovac replied:

> I know some departments include page numbers and also "black out" the redacted areas and/or put the sections of the Access to Information Act used to redact portions directly beside the information that has been removed. However, these are not requirements under the Act and it is not CBSA's practice to do this. We are required to advise you of the sections of the Act used to redact any information on the records and we do this by stating it in the letter we send you with the released records ... In a nut shell, this means that we do not advise you of where the redactions were made, but we do tell you what sections were used to redact information. If you have any concerns about what was redacted, you do have a right to complain to the Office of the Information Commissioner as detailed in the letter we sent you with the released records.

Pupovac's response demonstrates the ad hoc nature of ATI processing. By not revealing the number of redacted pages, or specifying which sections were invoked where and when, Pupovac exposes the ability of institutions to engage in practices that are clearly information-blocking, with no presumption or fear of accountability. Moreover, it demonstrates how different departments adopt different practices, making the use of ATI highly inconsistent across the federal government. On March 8, 2014, I submitted CBSA file A-2010-04262 to the OIC for a complaint regarding the content redactions. It remains to be investigated.

A useful tool that ATI users can use to counter some of these barriers is to "ATIP an ATIP" (Piché 2012; Walby and Larsen 2012). This tactic involves making a request on the processing of your initial request. Kevin Walby and Mike Larsen (2012: 36) have described this process as the "most important moment of reflexivity in ATI/FOI research, for if the goal is to understand how government agencies work with texts and manage information there is no better opportunity to investigate those issues than exploring the textual trails forged in relation to a previous request." Using this strategy, ATI users can receive a number of files pertaining to the processing of a request, including internal correspondence and correspondence with other departments regarding consultations. Most illuminating are the records from the AccessPro Case Management system that logs all activities (somewhat esoterically) that transpire on a file. Focusing on the file noted above (A-2010-04262), these AccessPro records highlight a number of problems with the procedural practices of ATI offices. It is important to note that this kind of information is not normally provided to requesters, even when they ask for detailed updates on the processing of their files. Noteworthy elements of this particular disclosure included:

1. A total of 89 pages were reviewed, 55 pages were released.

2. Full account of timelines: Days allowed 120, days taken 721.

3. The file was prepared for release in July 2011, but then additional documents were found. Wagdin wanted to release the records that were already prepared but was discouraged from doing so by manager Alain Belleville. A note in the AccessPro system states: "It was discovered during the Comms process that there were missing records—[Program bureau] needed to be tasked." Despite repeated queries on the status of the file, I was never told about the addition of new materials, and I was never informed that some records were completed and approved for release (nor was I given the option to receive a partial release, which is a common practice in other departments).

4. Consultations, which are normally the main reason for long delays, were completed rather promptly. After discovering the new documents, the package was sent to DFAIT, DND, and Public Safety in August 2011. DND and Public Safety Canada responded in September 2011 with no redactions. DFAIT responded in April 2012. According to AccessPro, all consultations were completed by April 2012.

5. File processing has a number of anomalies that indicate potential political interference. For example, AccessPro shows a long delay before the files were reviewed. Wagdin began reviewing the files on July 12, 2012, and completed the review (ahead of schedule) on August 21, 2012. With no reason provided, the file was transferred from Wagdin to senior manager Tara Rapley on September 21, 2012. Yet the files were not released until February 2013. Thus, there was a five-month gap with no notes or explanation.

6. Upon finalizing the package (for the second time), it was widely distributed for approvals. Pupovac sent the file to the communications staff for review, where communications officer Melanie Reasbeck replied: "This package is ok for release. No concern." The file was also distributed to senior managers in the issues management and communications teams, as well as the communications listserv. AccessPro also indicates (although no

emails were provided in the disclosure) that the ATI office was in communication with the minister's office: "MO Head's Up sent via email." The MO "heads up" was sent on February 6, and the package released on February 11.

7. Finally, when my complaint with the OIC was established on March 20, 2013, CBSA provided a very rapid response—by April 15, 2013. The contents of the response to the OIC are not displayed, and the OIC does not tell a complainant very much (the file has been stalled with the OIC ever since).

To summarize, information gleaned from the "ATIP of the ATIP" demonstrates a number of important facts about the request that would have remained hidden. Most immediately, the page volume of the request and its overall timeline are made explicit. It may also act as a registrar that suggests (and can sometimes demonstrate) significant anomalies. In this case, the time lags raise troubling questions about potential "amber-lighting" as well as the involvement of senior management. In short, this process reveals the sub-layers of activity that are involved in generating ATI information, and casts light on the numerous barriers that arise when requesting sensitive information.

Superficial and Arbitrary Document Retrieval

Issues of superficiality and arbitrariness permeate the ATI process. The two most important factors that contribute to superficial and arbitrary practices are poor document retrieval and redactions, both of which can figure into the non-disclosure of documents. Complaints arising from poor record retrieval and instances where records are exempted or excluded represent much of the overall workload of the OIC. This is particularly true with respect to security-related files. The non-disclosure of files represents a significant barrier to social science research because it compromises the ability of researchers to explore, report on, and interpret government programs and practices. Importantly, researchers can still report on the process of doing ATI research with the goal of informing future ATI users. This is particularly important when exploring social justice issues, where documents are being requested, yet departments are responding that "no records exist."

The OIC has detailed, on a number of occasions, how ATI offices are underfunded, under-resourced, and understaffed. These problems have been compounded by a general increase in ATI research and ATI requests, which is in part the result of the federal Conservatives' restrictive policies on communications and access to information. In addition to problems of money, staffing, and workload, the request process itself raises problems when ATI officers delegate the job of aggregating records. As demonstrated in the case of Linda Polowin at DFAIT, program areas might not be interested in turning over documents, might not know where documents are stored, and might hold general hostilities about being the subject of an ATI investigation. All of these factors can contribute to poor performance in the relaying of documents. In some cases where ATI users utilize "shotgun" requests that are very broad in scope, ATI offices can provide dismissive responses more easily. However, in cases where ATI users have knowledge of particular documents (or a strong indication that the documents exist), the superficiality of the ATI process becomes more evident.

To demonstrate, consider this series of requests involving the RCMP on training the Palestinian Civilian Police in the West Bank. On May 14, 2011, I requested documents related to RCMP support of the EUPOL COPPS mission, including "documents used for or during training sessions (handouts, reports, powerpoints)." I received the disclosure of 217 pages in January 2012 (RCMP 2011-0805). Although I asked for a number of specific documents, Monthly Reports are the lowest hanging fruit and as a result, they comprised a major component of the final release. In the reports, there were several documents that made reference to specific training programs, in particular a course called "policing in a democratic society." The notes from the reports indicated the dates and locations of the courses, the names of the RCMP facilitators, and reported/confirmed that the course was well received. In November 2013, I requested the following:

> All materials prepared for the Palestine Civilian Police course "policing in a democratic society"; 2) Mission Implementation Plan (MIP) for years 2008 to 2012; and 3) the assessment report turned over on 2009-01-16 by Canadian police trainers to the senior management of the EUPOL COPPS.

Several months later, I received an undated letter with a response that "no records exist." I wrote to ATI officer Dana McAteer to inquire about where the records might be located. As is often the case at the RCMP's ATI office, McAteer never replied. Instead of pursuing a complaint on this file, I opted to retry with the same department and (ideally) a different ATI officer. After submitting a new request, with the old content, I received a quick response in August 2014 that said the documents are EUPOL COPPS documents, and not under RCMP possession or control. I responded to ATI officer Francine Larose to explain that RCMP members on the deployment regularly use their RCMP emails to send Monthly Reports. Furthermore, using documents from my previous ATI request, I politely informed her that staff on Palestine deployment are issued RCMP laptops and are given directives to use those laptops in order "to stay current with matters in Canada." I asked Larose whether the "comprehensive" search had included any laptops, backup hard drives, or emails. She refused to answer and, regrettably, the file was sent to the OIC, where it remains.

Redactions

A number of recent cases have demonstrated that governments apply exemptions to records more broadly than is necessary, particularly with sensitive files. In many of these cases, the decision to withhold files is discretionary and based on a department's invocation of exemption authorities from the *Act*. Within the *ATIA*, there are two classes of exemptions: class-based exemptions and injury-based exemptions. Class-based exemptions are mandatory exemptions that relate to sections of the ATIA specifying that institutions "*shall* refuse to disclose" documents that correctly fall within its scope, whereas injury-based exemptions specify that institutions "*may* refuse to disclose" documents through discretionary criteria based on a standard of reasonableness (emphasis added). The distinction between these categories is summarized in *Bronskill v. Canada* 2012 (para 13):

> Class-based exemptions are typically involved when the nature of the documentation sought is sensitive in and of itself. For example, the section 13 exemption is related to information obtained from foreign governments, which, by its nature, is a class-based exemption. Injury-based exemptions require that the decision-maker analyze whether the release of information could be prejudicial to the interests articulated in the exemption. Section 15 is an injury-based exemption: the head of the government institution must assess whether the disclosure of information could "be expected to be injurious to the conduct of international affairs, the defence of Canada or any state allied or associated with Canada or the detection, prevention or suppression of subversive or hostile activities."

So, depending on the exemption provisions claimed, the government either has the obligation or the discretion to enforce an exemption. When ATI users file a complaint to investigate the overuse of exemption discretion, the OIC, and later the courts, have to evaluate the decision using a two-step process. First, it must be determined whether the records fall into the appropriate exemption provisions of the *Act* (standard of correctness), and then it must be determined whether the institution applied discretion appropriately (standard of reasonableness).[1]

To demonstrate that discretionary exemptions have been invoked reasonably, the responding institution must meet some high thresholds (in theory). Jurisprudence on ATI cases related to exemptions have required that they be "limited and specific" as well as demonstrate "reasonable expectation of probable harm" (see *Bronskill v. Canada* 2012). Recently in *Braunshweig v. Canada* (2012: para 56), it was ruled that "the explanation given to show the evaluation of the injury, if disclosure occurs, is serious, in depth, professional and factually based." Courts have also stressed that the evidence used to justify exemptions cannot be speculative, nor can redactions be invoked to prevent embarrassment or to hide illegal acts.

While the jurisprudence clearly underlines that the evidence required for an injury-based exemption must be based on clear, direct, and convincing evidence of harm, complaints arising from the overuse of discretionary exemptions are common and increasing. An illustrative case of discretionary redactions is the case of the Tommy Douglas files held by Library and Archives Canada (LAC). Tommy Douglas has been widely celebrated for his contributions to Canadian political life. A large body of literature has detailed how Douglas and other activists in the 1960s were routinely placed under surveillance by policing and security agencies. Although these campaigns against the political left are public knowledge, the national security files pertaining to Tommy Douglas have not been fully disclosed. Because Canada does not have a formal document declassification procedure, *Canadian Press* journalist Jim Bronskill filed an information request in 2005 with LAC (the files were transferred from the RCMP to the national archives) for a "copy of the RCMP Security Service File(s) on Thomas Clement (Tommy) Douglas."

With the files not forthcoming, Bronskill launched a complaint with the OIC (which subsequently investigated the matter) and in 2007 he filed for judicial review.[2] As a result, a number of inconsistencies that were not identified in the OIC investigation became apparent. While the OIC had found that both the national archives and the Canadian Security and Intelligence Service (CSIS) properly handled the files, litigation revealed that these institutions had, in fact, not turned over all the files in their possession. Litigating ATI files in the federal court can be a highly effective (but costly) mechanism of generating disclosure. Litigation affords the opportunity to investigate the actual processing steps of ATI requests. For example, it often includes ATI officers filing affidavits, which explain the institutional decisions regarding redactions or delays. If affidavits are filed, it also allows ATI users to cross-examine these officials under oath.

What emerged from the Tommy Douglas files was that LAC and CSIS had unilaterally limited the scope of the files to focus (very literally) on a specific "RCMP Security Service File," as opposed to a general recognition of files (plural) in their possession. The result was that a number of files that were referenced in the RCMP Security Service File were excluded. The court describes affidavits and testimonies from CSIS's ATI Coordinator Nicole Jalbert as "disingenuous." Likewise, it suggested that both Jalbert and Bill Wood, Acting Director of the Access to Information, Privacy and Personnel Records Division at LAC, acted in bad faith throughout the document retrieval and litigation process.

Although Bronskill's use of judicial review was successful in releasing a large volume of records that would have otherwise remained hidden, his efforts to release the full Tommy Douglas files were stalled at the Federal Court of Appeal (then failed to receive leave to appeal at the Supreme Court). As a result, 215 pages of the file remain forever sealed and other documents retain significant redactions. This case, and many others like it, demonstrate the highly discretionary process of ATI exemptions.

Conclusions: Motionless but Not Dead

Political interference, time delays and fees, poor document retrieval, and arbitrary redactions can make using ATI processes in Canada unpredictable and frustrating. In addition to these barriers, users have few forms of redress given the limitations of the OIC complaints process. In the long run, these and other shortcomings can only be addressed through legislative reforms. In the short term, however, there are ways to get around these barriers, many of which are addressed throughout this book. For instance, one useful strategy that I have used over the years is to send multiple requests to multiple departments. This can increase a researcher's chances of success and reduce the likelihood of impenetrable barriers. Of course, pursuing multiple requests is not without its own pitfalls. In many cases, department officials will have to consult with their colleagues in other departments if/when document materials require consultation. These consultations can be time-consuming and can result in more document suppression. It also requires that researchers have their own resources, which ideally will include a fixed address (for several years), time (potentially several years), money, and a lot of patience. Despite these limitations, however, multiple requests can be highly productive.

In the end, there is no magic formula to counter the barriers outlined in this chapter. Given the current framework of the *ATIA*, the best counter-strategy for ATI users is to be knowledgeable of the major barriers that exist, and then proceed with their research as strategically as possible. We should try to refrain from expecting one or two requests to turn up groundbreaking information and, instead, assume that ATI requests will be met with various barriers and inconsistencies. ATI requests are most useful when used as one tactic within a larger strategy of data collection. Thus, we should be supplementing our initial ATI requests with other strategies and tactics. ATI research can be frustrating, but it remains a crucial tool for critical researchers and social justice activism.

NOTES

1   See *Braunschweig v. Canada* (2014); *Ontario (Public Safety and Security) v. Criminal Lawyers' Association* (2010); *Attaran v. Canada* (2011).

2   After a complaint with the OIC, ATI users can proceed to Judicial Review (JR). Two options are available: 1) when the OIC believes the institution

has not adequately responded to their investigation, the OIC can take the file to JR on your behalf. While it is free for ATI users, the original requester has limited strategic involvement in the process. 2) If the OIC believes the complaint was resolved—and you contest this finding— a complainant can file their own JR. The Bronskill complaint is a recent example of the latter.

REFERENCES

Brewster, M. 2014. Harper Government Considers Soldiers on Viagra a Cabinet Secret: Cabinet Secrets Remain Sealed to the Public for 20 Years. *The Canadian Press*, September 14.

Fissin, D. 2013. *Enforcing Order: An Ethnography of Urban Policing.* London: Polity.

Hameed, Y. and J. Monaghan. 2012. Accessing Dirty Data: Methodological Strategies for Social Problems Researchers. In M. Larsen and K. Walby (eds.), *Brokering Access: Politics, Power and Freedom of Information in Canada.* Vancouver: UBC Press.

Office of the Information Commissioner (OIC). 2014. Annual Report 2013-2014. Ottawa.

_____. 2010. Special Report. At <oic-ci.gc.ca/eng/rp-pr_spe_rep_rap-spe_rep-car_fic-ren_2009-2010_all.aspx>

Piché, J. 2012. Accessing the State of Imprisonment in Canada: Information Barriers and Negotiation Strategies. In M. Larsen and K. Walby (eds.), *Brokering Access: Politics, Power and Freedom of Information in Canada.* Vancouver: UBC Press.

Pugliese, D. 2012. DND Tells Staff to Withhold Information; Move is to Protect Tories, Opposition Says. *Ottawa Citizen*, September 21.

Rees, A. 2012. Sustaining Secrecy: Executive Branch Resistance to Access to Information in Canada. In M. Larsen and K. Walby (eds.), *Brokering Access: Politics, Power and Freedom of Information in Canada.* Vancouver: UBC Press.

_____. 2003. Red File Alert: Public Access at Risk; Federal Surveillance System Flags Files—Ministries, Privy Council Delay Requests. *Toronto Star*, November 1.

Thompson, E. 2006. PS Brass Get 'Heads Up' over Access Releases. *Ottawa Citizen*, October 2.

Walby, K. and M. Larsen. 2012. Access to Information and Freedom of Information Requests: Neglected Means of Data Production in the Social Sciences. *Qualitative Inquiry* 18(1): 31-42.

LEGAL CASES

Attaran v. Canada (Minister of Foreign Affairs), 2011 FCA 182.
Braunschweig v. Canada (Minister of Public Safety), 2014 FC 218.
Bronskill v. Canada, 2011 FC 983.
Ontario (Public Safety and Security) v. *Criminal Lawyers' Association*, 2010 SCC 23.

CHAPTER 4

USING ACCESS TO INFORMATION TO SEPARATE OIL AND STATE IN CANADA

Keith Stewart and Kyla Tanner

A core part of Greenpeace Canada's climate and energy campaign is to expose how the alliance between the oil industry and the federal government impedes effective action on climate change. Despite its shortcomings, Access to Information (ATI) legislation has proven to be a powerful tool in our quest at Greenpeace to separate oil and state. By enabling a peek behind the curtain that often hides the discussions between the oil industry and the federal government, we can uncover the influence of corporate lobbyists and spark an open debate on what is actually in the national interest.

Though Greenpeace is best known for its high-profile protests, investigative research into environmentally and socially harmful practices has been an important part of our campaigns over the last 40 years. For example, we have done groundbreaking work to trace the "chain of custody" for various products so that consumers know how the products were made. We have also played a key role in exposing and publicizing the funding of "climate denial" networks by fossil fuel companies (Greenpeace USA 2013). Indeed, it was Greenpeace that first published research on the secret funding of front groups and think tanks by Koch Industries (Greenpeace USA 2010). This muckraking research on the political activities of corporations to delay or prevent action on climate change has been paired with more solutions-oriented research. For instance, we have worked with the renewable energy sector and outside experts to develop detailed blueprints for transitioning from fossil fuels and nuclear power to more renewable energy systems.[1] Greenpeace's Energy [R]evolution work is so technically sophisticated that it was selected by the Intergovernmental Panel on Climate Change (IPCC) as one of the four lead scenarios in the IPCC's 2011 Special Report on Renewable Energy and Climate Change Mitigation (Edenhofer et al. 2011).

Even the best information does not, on its own, result in social change. Research by Greenpeace and the IPCC, among others, has consistently found that there is no technological or economic reason why we cannot make a rapid transition off of fossil fuels to avoid the worst impacts of climate change. The key barrier is what is euphemistically called a lack of political will to implement the policies necessary to effect this transition. Despite the scientific consensus that carbon emissions need to be rapidly reduced—and the solid understanding that exists about how to make that happen—governments continue to defend and promote short-term corporate interests over the public interest. While solutions do exist, their deployment is held back by a combination of institutional inertia, corporate political power, and the policies and relationships that favour conventional energy extraction. For Greenpeace, any strategy that seeks to implement solutions to the climate crisis without also shifting this balance of political power will not be successful. If not successfully challenged, this power imbalance will be reinforced as cascading climate and other disruptions accelerate. We are hardly alone in our assessment that one of the most significant barriers to action on climate change is the immense political power of the companies that benefit from the energy status quo (see Hayes 2014; McKibben 2012). The question quickly becomes: what can we do about it?

Separating Oil and State

This is where the concept of separating oil and state comes in. By exposing the close ties between governments and industry, and then subjecting the resulting policy decisions to public scrutiny, we can help reduce the power of the fossil fuel industry in Canada. Pursuing information and evidence using the tools created by the various Canadian access to information and privacy acts has been vital to this work (although in our usual brazen style, Greenpeace Canada also hung a huge banner that read "Separate Oil and State" off of the tallest tower in Calgary in 2010). In some countries, the power of the fossil fuel industry is expressed through the direct corporate funding of politicians and political parties. This is less important in Canada, where at the federal level at least campaign finance laws put limits on this form of influence. There is, however, a systemic ideological bias on the part of corporate Canada,[2] our major media outlets, and our major political parties that what is good for the oil companies is good for the country as a whole.

As a former member of the Prime Minister's Office under Stephen Harper told one of the authors: "This is a government that sees the oil industry as its partner in achieving its vision of what the country should be. You [environmentalists] are the enemy."[3] This view was expressed publicly in a 2012 open letter from then Natural Resources Minister Joe Oliver. The letter was published the day before hearings into the Northern Gateway pipeline began. It included the following rationale for changes to the regulatory process that would limit public input and grant greater discretion to the federal cabinet, which was subsequently implemented as part of an omnibus budget bill:

> Unfortunately, there are environmental and other radical groups
> that would seek to block this opportunity to diversify our trade.
> Their goal is to stop any major project no matter what the cost
> to Canadian families in lost jobs and economic growth. No for-
> estry. No mining. No oil. No gas. No more hydro-electric dams.
> These groups threaten to hijack our regulatory system to achieve
> their radical ideological agenda. They seek to exploit any loophole
> they can find, stacking public hearings with bodies to ensure that
> delays kill good projects. They use funding from foreign special

interest groups to undermine Canada's national economic interest. They attract jet-setting celebrities with some of the largest personal carbon footprints in the world to lecture Canadians not to develop our natural resources. Finally, if all other avenues have failed, they will take a quintessential American approach: sue everyone and anyone to delay the project even further. They do this because they know it can work. It works because it helps them to achieve their ultimate objective: delay a project to the point it becomes economically unviable (Oliver 2012).

This assumption that what is good for the extractive industries is ultimately in the "national interest" (and that those who challenge this economic agenda are "enemies" of Canada) is part of what we set out to challenge.

Why Use Access to Information?

One of the great things about pursuing information via ATI is that it can get activists out of policy-wonk mode (where we try to tell people why they should be interested in something they are not) and into storytelling mode. It is not enough for environmentalists to simply assert that the public interest is different from what the government claims it is. To broaden the debate beyond our existing supporters (who, by and large, already agree with us on this point), we determined that we needed to shift the terms of public debate by changing the frame of mainstream media stories from "environmentalists claim that..." to "documents obtained under access to information show that...." Everyone loves to know a good secret, so by framing the story as revealing a sensational detail, or as something that was kept hidden, we can capture an audience's attention. Oftentimes an audience already suspects what you will reveal (e.g., governments listen to oil companies more than average citizens), but with confidential internal documents in hand we can now conclusively demonstrate that it is true.

Sometimes a little luck is involved. For example, a few weeks after Minister Oliver released his "radicals" letter in 2012, Greenpeace managed to get a copy of the federal government's "Oil Sands Advocacy Strategy." We had received heavily redacted versions of this plan before, but in this instance the column headings were not redacted (in our opinion, they never should have been redacted). The column headings identified various groups as either "allies" (oil companies, the chamber of commerce, the National Energy Board) or "adversaries" (environmental and Indigenous groups, some media) in the Canadian government's efforts to block the European Fuel Quality directive that would have required reductions in greenhouse gas emissions from transport fuels (and thus limited tar sands imports into Europe). This exposure resulted in national news coverage (see Fitzgerald 2012) and provided solid evidence that the federal government was siding with oil companies to lobby against environmental laws in other countries.

The strategic and persistent use of ATI can help level the playing field when it comes to shifting public opinion. Environmental and Indigenous groups will never be able to match the advertising budgets of the oil industry or federal government, but access to information legislation can help broaden democratic debate beyond government and industry talking points. This argument was eloquently summed up by *Calgary Herald* business columnist Stephen Ewart (2013):

> There are two distinct dialogues happening these days encompassing governments, the oil industry and Canadians. You can hardly avoid one of the conversations—it's advertised on TV and other media 24/7. It is the other discussion that takes more effort to observe. That's because it relies on environmentalists and/or journalists using federal and provincial access to information laws to get a peek at the ongoing dialogue between the oil industry and governments. Both contribute to overall energy literacy in Canada.

Ewart singled out the work of Greenpeace and the Pembina Institute in using these tools to inform public debate, and argued that it is actually in the government's interest to strengthen them:

> Freedom of information requests may be the bane of oil and gas lobbyists or government bureaucrats but they aren't synonymous with the WikiLeaks saga. As Suzanne Legault, information commissioner of Canada, said recently, access to government information is an expression of Canadians' core values and 'fundamental to the functioning of democracy.' Legault called on Ottawa to put controls on instant text messages from civil servants—in particular ministers' office staff—this week to preserve government records and respect the access to information law. There are numerous calls for Ottawa to update the 30-year-old Access to Information law and there's logic to it. Since it's proving to be one of the better communication tools in understanding what's happening with public policy and the oil and gas sector it would even help industry and governments realize their goal of increasing energy literacy … And it doesn't include spending a fortune on ads.

Even when there is not any breaking news in documents received, a sidebenefit of ATI requests is the fact that civil servants typically produce detailed briefing notes. These memos contain both useful data and the policy options being considered, which can inform the strategy of social activists. For example, civil servants typically prepare scenario notes for meetings, which identify the key points the minister or deputy minister should convey to the third party, as well as questions they may be asked and the answers that should be provided. The ATI package may also include communications from industry such as emails, letters, PowerPoint presentations, and reports, which provide details on what the industry lobbyists are telling, and asking of, government decision-makers. Pieces of information that you will not receive are advice to ministers, advice to cabinet, and many things covered by specific rules, such as corporate information relating to competition concerns, private information of individuals, and material not relevant to your specific request. This type of information will be redacted from the documents that you receive, literally blocked out so you are unable to read it. Understanding how to specify and narrow your request will help you to avoid these problems.

The irony soon confronted by anyone using ATI is that it works best if you know precisely what document you want. Searches with vague parameters can cost a lot of money because it will take a great deal of time for them to gather your requested information (at the federal level, each request gets five hours of free search time, and after that you pay per hour). For example, a Greenpeace request to the Alberta government under its Freedom of Information legislation for records relating to lobbying on tar sands-related regulations by Shell came back with a cost estimate of over $23,000. One quick and inexpensive way to gather information is to request copies of ATI documents that have already been gathered. Every government department has a list of the completed ATI requests on its web page. You can get copies of these completed ATI documents for free in a matter of only a few weeks. This can be useful for building up your research file, but whoever originally requested the information has probably already leaked any of the document's juicy material to the media.

Our campaign's primary technique to tighten up searches was to go through the federal lobbyist registry database to determine the precise dates when representatives of the oil industry met with federal officials (who are identified by name in the database) and then submit requests for all records related to those meetings. This proved to be productive initially, but less so as government and industry officials recognized what we were doing and simply stopped generating records accessible through ATI (we have since filed a complaint with the Information Commissioner relating to 31 meetings we requested in 2013 between senior officials and industry that came back as "no records found").

The fact that these meetings took place is relatively uninteresting on its own. Our goal was to gain access to the communications that took place before the meetings, what was on the agenda, the talking points established in advance, as well as what was communicated and agreed upon between the two parties during the meetings (minutes, presentations made, etc.). One of the reasons we pursued documentation of meetings with lobbyists was that we judged it less likely to be redacted (an assumption that would appear to have been correct, based on a comparison with other ATI requests). There are two principal reasons for this. First, some of the information has already been shared outside of government. The contents of briefing notes is often redacted because it is deemed to be advice to the minister or confidential in some other way, but the information in scenario notes prepared for meetings with third parties is intended to be shared with outsiders. So, while some of the background can be (and usually is) redacted, the government's position is often displayed in the sections dealing with "main points to register" (the key points the government representative should be sure to convey to the group they are meeting with) or in the prepared answers to questions that may be asked. Secondly, the material shared by the corporate representatives with the government representatives (e.g., PowerPoint presentations, letters requesting the meeting) can usually only be redacted if deemed to be commercially confidential.

With limited time and money, there was no way we could pursue the documentation of all the meetings between oil industry representatives and the federal government. According to the Polaris Institute, the oil industry met 2,733 times with federal officials between July 2008 and November 2012 (Cayley-Daoust and Girard 2012). Given the limited information in the lobbyist registry on what the meetings were about, we focused our requests on specific Designated Public Office Holders (e.g., cabinet ministers or civil servants responsible for an area we were interested in) and time periods, such as the lead-up to the 2012 omnibus budget bill.

Over the course of two years, Greenpeace's climate and energy campaign submitted over 100 ATI requests related to meetings with oil industry lobbyists, as well as dozens of other general requests such as "all information relating to the transport of bitumen by rail." These requests have generated dozens of media stories on a wide variety of topics. Below, we focus on two case studies to illustrate how we have used this research strategy.

Case Study I: Oil Industry Lobbying and Environmental Deregulation in the 2012 Omnibus Budget Bill

The 2012 federal budget was remarkable in the depth and breadth of changes to Canada's environmental laws. Coming in the aftermath of Minister Oliver's "radicals" letter cited above, it included over 150 pages of changes to environmental laws. Omnibus bills of this type are popular for "hiding" the changes within them. Of the many amendments introduced in the bill, those that most concerned the environment involved a complete overhaul of the *Canadian Environmental Assessment Act* (CEAA) 1995. CEAA 1995 was replaced with CEAA 2012, which streamlined processes with far fewer triggers and limited the scope of environmental assessments. A narrowing of scope allowed for these assessments to focus only on one aspect of a mining project, for example, instead of all of the anticipated impacts. The budget legislation forced the Canadian Environmental Assessment Agency to cancel nearly 3,000 screenings (MacCharles 2012). Of these, 678 involved fossil fuel energy and 248 involved a pipeline. Fish habitat protection was severely weakened by amendments to the *Fisheries Act*, specifically section 35. The amendments expanded the authorization for harm and narrowed prohibition against harm. Also, approvals issued under the *Navigable Waters Protection Act* (NWPA) no longer triggered a federal environmental assessment.

In December 2012, a second budget implementation bill altered the NWPA, renaming it the *Navigation Protection Act* (NPA). The NPA includes three oceans, 97 lakes, and portions of 62 rivers. By comparison, Canada is estimated to contain nearly 32,000 major lakes and more than 2.25 million rivers. This means that the NPA excludes 99.7 percent of Canada's lakes and more than 99.9 percent of its rivers from federal oversight. Notably absent from the proposed schedule are significant rivers in British Columbia, such as the Kitimat and Upper Fraser Rivers, which lie along the path of the proposed Northern Gateway pipeline. Major pipelines are exempt under the new law, meaning the scope of impacts considered during environmental reviews is narrower.

The government's official position is that these changes eliminate "red tape" and reduce the regulatory burden on business. But the more nakedly political motives were made clear when Environment Minister Peter Kent claimed that Canadian environmental groups concerned about the expansion of the tar sands were being "used to launder off-shore foreign funds" (Paris 2012). This allegation was used to justify new rules in the budget bill designed to crack down on politically active charities, along with allocating $8 million for stepped-up audits of charities engaged in advocacy. The government argued that these changes were in the national interest, while Greenpeace and other environmental groups argued that they were primarily in the interest of the oil industry. In order to back up this claim, Greenpeace submitted multiple ATI requests targeting meetings between the oil industry and federal officials in the lead-up to the 2012 omnibus budget bill. As a result of these requests, we discovered that in October 2011 the Canadian Energy Pipelines Association (CEPA) arranged a meeting to lobby top foreign affairs officials. A CEPA slide show presentation from the meeting stated that they were "strong advocates for regulatory reform" and were pursuing "changes to the Canadian Environmental Assessment Act and [n]ew regulations under Navigable Waters Protection Act." CEPA also expressed their "desire to collaborate with the federal government to create a framework that will enable timely development of critical energy infrastructure to ensure Canada remains competitive in a global energy marketplace."[4]

Following this meeting, the Canadian Association of Petroleum Producers, CEPA, and the Canadian Petroleum Products Institute sent a joint letter to Environment Minister Peter Kent and Natural Resource Minister Joe Oliver:

> The purpose of our letter is to express our shared views on the near-term opportunities before the government to address regulatory reform for major energy industries in Canada. ...[W]e believe that the basic approach embodied in existing legislation is out-dated. At the heart of most existing legislation is a philosophy of prohibiting harm; "environmental" legislation is almost entirely focused on preventing bad things from happening rather than enabling responsible outcomes. This results in a position of adversarial prohibition, rather than enabling collaborative conservation to achieve agreed common goals.

The industry letter identified six acts that were "outdated" and too restrictive: the *National Energy Board Act, Canadian Environmental Assessment Act, Fisheries Act, Navigable Waters Protection Act, Species at Risk Act,* and the *Migratory Birds Convention Act.* The first four of these were subsequently amended along the lines requested by the oil industry, and the government indicated that the *Species at Risk Act* would be amended in the future. Greenpeace released these documents to the media, generating both television and print coverage (*CBC News* 2013; Scoffield 2013). It also shaped subsequent coverage, with the media asserting that the government implemented changes to environmental laws requested by industry as a matter of fact, rather than as a claim by environmentalists.

This coverage has, in turn, contributed to the undermining of the "social licence"[5] of both the oil industry and government regulators, as increasing numbers of citizens feel that the government has gone from being a neutral arbiter or "referee" between environmentalists and industry to being a cheerleader for Big Oil. The legitimacy of the approvals process requires at least the appearance of fairness, where both sides are able to put forward their arguments before a neutral decision-maker. When the rules are changed in the middle of the game, at the behest of one side, this sense of fairness is lost. The loss of social licence is reflected in the rise of opposition to pipeline proposals. This growing public opposition has triggered a significant increase in advertising spending by the oil industry and the federal government on "responsible resource development" to try to regain legitimacy.

The use of ATI is only one element in a multi-faceted struggle. In this case, it contributed to that struggle by exposing the behind-the-scenes collusion of government and industry, thereby shifting the terms of the debate about whose interests are really being served by these projects and legislative changes.

Case Study II: Transporting Oil by Rail and the Public Interest

The case of oil-by-rail demonstrates how ATI can be a powerful tool for exposing lax government oversight and the subordination of public safety to corporate interests in government policy-making. Greenpeace first became aware of the increasing amounts of oil moving by rail in January 2013 because of a story in *The Globe and Mail* (Vanderklippe 2013). There was very little publicly available information on this new trend, so in February we began submitting ATI requests to see what discussions were taking place within the federal government, as well as between the government and the rail industry.

While awaiting responses to those requests (we have found that it usually takes three to six months, sometimes more than a year, to get a response to an ATI request), we identified safety issues with the rail cars being used to transport the oil. As far back as the early 1990s, the Transportation Safety Board of Canada (1994) noted issues with the 111A tank cars, stating that: "The susceptibility of 111A tank cars to release product at derailment and impact is well documented. The transport of a variety of the most hazardous products in such cars continues." These warnings have continued in the past two decades and have been echoed by the National Transportation Safety Board (2009) in the US. In 2009, there were only 500 carloads of crude oil moved by rail in Canada, but this increased to approximately 160,000 in 2013 (Transportation Safety Board of Canada 2014). With such a massive increase in the quantity of oil being moved, Greenpeace sought to draw attention to the increasing level of risk (Stewart 2013a). Our blog post on the railcar safety issue—written six weeks before the Lac-Mégantic disaster—ended with this line: "So the question is: if the Prime Minister is concerned over the safety of moving oil by rail, will he require companies moving hazardous products like crude oil or bitumen (and other toxic products) to avoid using DOT-111 tanker cars? Or is he willing to cut corners on safety in order to get oil to market, no matter what the cost?"

In the aftermath of the Lac-Mégantic tragedy, where 47 lives were lost when an oil train derailed and exploded, Greenpeace Canada did dozens of media interviews—as one of the few groups that had researched or written about oil-by-rail. This meant we were already established as an organization with expertise in this area once the responses to our ATI requests began to roll in shortly after Lac-Mégantic. What these documents showed was that the Harper government's primary focus was on gaining access to new markets in order to increase the amount of money oil companies received per barrel. Alberta oil was selling at a discount because of a lack of pipeline capacity, so the government was looking to increase the movement of oil by rail. In doing so, they turned a blind eye to the recommendations of their own safety experts.

For example, a 2013 memo entitled *Transporting Crude Oil by Rail* prepared for Natural Resources Minister Joe Oliver does not mention the issue of safety. In fact, it focuses almost exclusively on the role rail can play in reducing the price discount facing

Alberta's industry. The memo states that "NRCan is currently meeting with Transport Canada to mutually understand how rail can be part of a solution to current market access challenges."[6] A separate memo called *Potential for Oil by Rail* that was prepared for Ed Fast, Minister for the Asia-Pacific Gateway, and Denis Lebel, Minister of Transport, Infrastructure and Communities, did address the issue of safety, but stated that there were no major concerns:

> TC [Transport Canada] has identified no major safety concerns with the increased oil on rail capacity in Canada, nor with the safety of tank cars that are designed, maintained, qualified and used according to Canadian and US standards and regulations. Indeed, Canada and the US work collaboratively to ensure the harmonization of rail safety requirements. The transportation of oil by rail does not trigger the need for a federal environmental assessment under the Canadian Environmental Assessment Act (CEAA), however, proposals to construct new infrastructure to support the activity may be required to determine CEAA's applicability.[7]

This stands in stark contrast to the multiple and serious warnings from the Transportation Safety Board. Greenpeace publicized this information, leading to uncomfortable questions for the Minister of Transport (De Souza 2013). We also organized a joint call from more than 50 organizations for an end to the use of the model IIIA tank cars as well as a comprehensive public review of how we move and use oil in this country.

The industry's push for self-regulation initially took a blow when a separate set of documents obtained under ATI revealed that CN Rail was lobbying against the new safety measures brought in post-Lac-Mégantic (Bronskill and Cheadle 2014). Later, Greenpeace made front-page news when we revealed that there were behind-the-scenes negotiations over a major new oil-by-rail line through northern British Columbia (Cheadle 2013a). In this case, we used the lobbyist registry to discover that there had been a meeting between

Natural Resources Canada Deputy Minister Michael Keenan and CN Rail assistant vice president David Miller in April 2013. Through an ATI request we discovered that at this meeting, the two parties discussed how the Chinese-owned oil company Nexen was working with CN to examine the transportation of crude oil on CN's railway to Prince Rupert to be loaded onto tankers for export to Asia. The documents show that the federal government was clearly supportive of this proposal, and the PowerPoint presentation by CN Rail officials highlighted how this project could match (and thus potentially replace) the capacity of the controversial Northern Gateway Pipeline.[8]

From the perspective of its promoters, one of the key advantages of oil-by-rail (as noted above in the memo from Transport Canada) is that unlike pipelines, there are no significant approval processes required. By publicly revealing the proposal to ship up to seven trains per day (each with 100 carloads of oil) from Alberta to Prince Rupert, we were able to give communities a chance to respond to this initiative before it could be announced as a *fait accompli*. Overall, we were successful in challenging the initial response from government and industry that the Lac-Mégantic tragedy was solely the result of a human error that no one could have anticipated or prevented. We were able to demonstrate that warnings were ignored and that the expansion of oil-by-rail was still being actively pursued in spite of the known risks. Yet, our work in this area also ran into challenges. The default position of many observers is to frame the debate as a choice between rail and pipelines to move ever-increasing amounts of oil—a framing that has been encouraged by pipeline companies. In this context, Greenpeace's revelation that oil-by-rail is unsafe was often co-opted as an argument in favour of pipelines (see, for example, McPharland 2013).

Of course, this argument would have been made regardless of our ATI work; the tragic deaths of 47 people at Lac-Mégantic ensured that. And we consistently try to reframe the debate as a choice between investing in new dirty energy infrastructure (the pipelines or railcars required to expand tar sands production) and investing in clean energy, whether in an op-ed piece in the *Toronto Star* (Stewart 2013b) or in individual media stories like this *Canadian Press* article:

> Keith Stewart of Greenpeace Canada says the Lac-Megantic crash and some of the older pipeline spills show "a prioritizing of getting the oil out as quickly as possible over public safety and environmental safety." The argument of necessity for using the older, unsafe tank cars doesn't wash, said Stewart. "There is no constitutional right to move oil by any means necessary," he said in an interview. "That's a decision that Canadians get to make about what's safe enough to go through the heart of our communities; not the oil companies and not the rail companies." "If that means you're going to slow down that oil-by-rail revolution, well then it should be slowed down." (Cheadle 2013b)

Unfortunately, this kind of questioning of the basic premise of the debate (oil must get to market) is at best an afterthought in most media coverage. And since this kind of alternative (put community safety first) is not even considered by government or industry officials as an option, it will not appear in ATI documents. As a result, advocates are often left in the position of trying to communicate on what is *not* in the documents. The difficult work, then, is to use ATI materials to expose the alliance between the federal government and the oil lobby while not losing sight of the need to change the terms of the debate about oil and energy in Canada.

Conclusion

Environmental and social justice organizations are never going to be able to match the backroom lobbying power or advertising budgets of major corporations. We have to rely on "people power" to counter the financial and institutional power of the fossil fuel industry. Using ATI to expose the intimate relationship between governments and industry can help us build that power. It enables us to tell a compelling story about who benefits and who loses from government decisions in a way that speaks to people's sense of justice and concern for the welfare of the community. By allowing us partial access to the back-stage world of elite decision-making, we shift the debate back into the public sphere where social movements are strongest.

ATI also helps to reframe the debate; it allows activist organizations the opportunity to create the story rather than simply respond to what government or industry is saying. In Greenpeace's experience, ATI has proven to be a formidable counter to the Harper government's well-documented efforts to limit and control the flow of information. Indeed, this reputation for secrecy and control has increased the public and media appetite for details on what the government is trying to hide. ATI opens a window for light to shine into the backrooms of power. We should take advantage of it.

NOTES

1   You can find the results of the global and national Energy [R]evolution scenario modelling work at <energyblueprint.info>

2   See, for example, the 2013 report entitled "50 Million a Day" where the Canadian Chamber of Commerce argues that the lack of pipeline infrastructure to move oil sands bitumen to market is costing Canada $50 million per day in forgone revenue. At <chamber.ca/media/blog/130917-50-Million-a-Day/>

3   Personal communication with Keith Stewart. Not for attribution.

4   These ATI documents are available on the Greenpeace website at: <greenpeace.org/canada/en/Blog/oil-companies-may-regret-gutting-canadas-envi/blog/44028/>

5   Broadly speaking, "social licence" means that an organization's operations or projects have earned and maintained community, government, and First Nations' support. As environmental laws are weakened, having a permit from the government is no longer seen as sufficient for granting social licence to many resource development projects.

6   Documents available on the Greenpeace website: <greenpeace.org/canada/en/Blog/transport-canada-downplayed-risks-of-shipping/blog/46050/>

7 Documents available on the Greenpeace website: <greenpeace.org/
   canada/en/Blog/transport-canada-downplayed-risks-of-shipping/
   blog/46050/>

8 Documents available on the Greenpeace website: <greenpeace.org/
   canada/en/Blog/cn-rail-and-nexen-planning-gateway-sized-virt/
   blog/46725/>

REFERENCES

Bronskill, J. and B. Cheadle. 2014. CN Rail Opposed Emergency Rules
   After Lac-Megantic Blast: Documents. *The Canadian Press*, January 10.

Cayley-Daoust, D. and R. Girard. 2012. Big Oil's Oily Grasp. Ottawa:
   Polaris Institute.

CBC News. 2013. Energy Industry Letter Suggested Environmental Law
   Changes: Greenpeace Says Oil and Gas Companies Got What They
   Wanted from Ottawa. January 9.

Cheadle, B. 2013a. CN, Feds Eyeing Oil-By-Rail to Prince Rupert in Same
   Quantity as Gateway. *The Canadian Press*, September 22.

_____. 2013b. Oil Leads to Boom in Rail Tank-Car Business. *The Canadian
   Press*, July 10.

De Souza, M. 2013. Transport Canada Introduces Emergency Rules for
   Rail Safety Following Quebec Train Disaster. *Postmedia News*, July 23.

Edenhofer, O. et al. 2011. *IPCC Special Report on Renewable Energy and
   Climate Change Mitigation*. Cambridge: Cambridge University Press.

Ewart, S. 2013. Dual Energy Dialogues Provide Insight to Canadians.
   Calgary Herald, December 2.

Fitzgerald, M. 2012. Oilsands 'Allies' and 'Adversaries' Named in Federal
   Document. *CBC News*, January 26.

Greenpeace USA. 2013. Dealing in Doubt: The Climate Denial Machine
   versus Climate Science. At <greenpeace.org/usa/en/campaigns/
   global-warming-and-energy/polluterwatch/Dealing-in-Doubt
   ---the-Climate-Denial-Machine-vs-Climate-Science/>

_____. 2010. Koch Industries: Secretly Funding the Climate Denial
   Machine. At < greenpeace.org/usa/en/media-center/reports/
   koch-industries-secretly-fund/>

Hayes, C. 2014. The New Abolitionism. *The Nation*, May 12.

MacCharles, T. 2012. Tories have Cancelled Almost 600 Environmental
   Assessments in Ontario. *Toronto Star*, August 29.

McKibben, B. 2012. Global Warming's Terrifying New Math. *Rolling Stone*, July 19.

McPharland, K. 2013. A Light Bulb Finally Goes on at Greenpeace. *National Post*, September 24.

National Transportation Safety Board. 2009. Railroad Accident Report – Derailment of CN Freight Train U70691-18 with Subsequent Hazardous Materials Release and Fire, June 19.

Oliver, J. 2012. An Open Letter from the Honourable Joe Oliver, Minister of Natural Resources, on Canada's Commitment to Diversify our Energy Markets and the Need to Further Streamline the Regulatory Process in Order to Advance Canada's National Economic Interest, January 9.

Paris, M. 2012. Charities Urge Peter Kent to Retract 'Laundering' Accusation. *CBC News*, May 4.

Scoffield, H. 2013. Pipeline Industry Drove Changes to Navigable Waters Protection Act, Documents Show. *The Canadian Press*, February 20.

Stewart, K. 2013a. Boom in Rail Oil Shipments Rest on Unsafe Tanker Cars. *Toronto Star*, July 9.

_____. 2013b. Is the Oil Industry Using Unsafe Rail Cars to Transport Crude? At <greenpeace.org/canada/en/Blog/is-the-oil-industry-using-unsafe-rail-cars-to/blog/45237/>

Transportation Safety Board of Canada. 2014. Rail Recommendations R14-01, R14-02, R14-03, January 23.

_____. 1994. Railway Investigation Report R94T0029, January 30.

Vanderklippe, N. 2013. With Pipelines Under Attack, Railways Lead Race to Move Oil. *The Globe and Mail*, January 12.

CHAPTER 5

GAMES "BUREAUCATS" PLAY

Franke James

Why play games with "Bureaucats"?
What have you got to win?

Well, you have lots to win. That's what makes the game so fascinating and fun. I am quite sure that the Canadian government loathes my upbeat attitude. Filing access to information (ATI) requests is supposed to make your eyes glaze over as you nod off to sleep. They don't want you relishing the task with gusto or glee. And they certainly do not want people revealing the tricks they play on unwary citizens. I chuckle as I imagine them using *Games Bureaucats Play* as a cautionary tale on what bureaucrats should NEVER get caught doing—lest the truth leak out and they be held up to public ridicule. But before you dive into the games, let me tell you the backstory on how they came to be.

Four years ago I didn't know anything about access to information requests. I had no inkling I would ever need to learn about them. But on May 19, 2011, everything changed. That was the day that I spoke with Sandra Antonovic, the director of an educational non-profit organization in Croatia called Nektarina. Antonovic was organizing a touring exhibition of my climate change art in Europe. Its goal was to inspire students to create their own climate change art and take action on reducing their carbon footprint. Sounds great, right?

2,172 ATI PAGES

Franke James received 2,172 pages of documents from the Canadian government, released under the Access to Information and Privacy Act, which were related to her and her work as an environmental artist.

Department of Foreign Affairs (DFAIT)
- A-2011-00802: 581 pages (October 2011-February 2012)
- A-2011-01800: 976 pages (April 2012)
- A-2012-02002: 193 pages (November 2012)
- A-2012-02946: 41 pages (February 2013)

Environment Canada
- A-2012-01156: 149 pages (March 2013)

Ministry Of Natural Resources (ATI and Privacy Act)
- DC7040-12-276 and DC7050-12-10: 157 pages (November 2012)

Privy Council
- A-2011-00009: 38 pages (July 2012)
- A-2012-00407: 26 pages (November 2012)
- A-2012-00695: 11 pages (March 2013)

The official secretly WARNED NEKTARINA NOT to EXHIBIT my ART

"DON'T YOU KNOW this ARTIST Speaks AGAINST the CANADIAN GOVERNMENT??"

The PROOF given was my "DEAR PRIME MINISTER" essay about a CARBON TAX!

which is reaLLY SHOCKING...

But that day in mid-May she had bad news to share with me. She told me she had submitted a funding proposal to the Canadian embassy in Croatia. This was a surprise to me—but in fact Canada is one of the signatories on the United Nations Framework Convention on Climate Change (UNFCCC) agreement to provide advocacy funds to organizations around the world for local climate change education.

The bad news was that although $5,000 in advocacy funds had been approved in writing by the Department of Foreign Affairs (DFAIT), the funds were now being cancelled. Antonovic met with Vlatka Ljubenko, the Canadian embassy cultural officer at a coffee shop in Croatia. Antonovic told me that Ljubenko warned her not to show my art saying, "This is off the record ... Don't you know this artist speaks against the Canadian government?"

I was flabbergasted and asked why this cultural officer would tell her that. Antonovic said, "Oh, Ottawa is very unhappy with your visual essay to the Prime Minister." (In 2008, I had written an online visual essay to Prime Minister Harper asking for a carbon tax. Perhaps naively, I never expected retaliation from Ottawa for speaking my mind.) Antonovic also told me that when a senior official in Ottawa heard that the advocacy funds were to be used to exhibit my climate change art, he exclaimed, "Who's the idiot who approved of an art show by that woman, Franke James?"

Well, that was it. I now had a burning desire to find out what those bureaucats were saying about me behind the scenes—and how and why they were warning people not to support me. Aren't all Canadians equal? Why should I be treated differently than other Canadian artists, authors, and citizens who get a friendly handshake from embassy staff?

I considered filing ATI requests, but I didn't do it. I'd never filed one before, and I talked myself out of it, assuming they would not yield anything valuable.

Instead, I decided to write to the Canadian embassies in Europe and ask if I could rent space for events around my touring show. Initially the response was very positive, with embassy staff telling me they'd like to help me. But then I received the official word by email saying that they regretted they could not be of assistance. It was abundantly clear that no Canadian embassy wanted anything to do with me.

By July 2011, the media had got wind of my dilemma. Tonda MacCharles, at the *Toronto Star*, interviewed Sandra Antonovic, me, and Jean-François Lacelle, a spokesperson from the Canadian government. The article, "Artist sees red over government blacklisting," was published on July 28, 2011. Antonovic's statements (which included the "Don't you know this artist speaks against the Canadian government?" and the "Who's the idiot" quote) were contrasted with the flat-out denials Lacelle sent by email. He wrote, "Funding was never withdrawn, nor was it guaranteed." Amy Chung at the *National Post* also wrote about my blacklisting, and she included more denials by the government. Foreign Affairs spokesman Chris Day was quoted saying, "No money was ever guaranteed nor was it withdrawn."

I knew that the government was misleading the media—but I did not have the documents to prove it. I only had Antonovic's word that the Canadian government was warning people not to support me, and that they had withdrawn the funding. In phone calls, Antonovic told me she felt bullied and that her small non-profit could not withstand the intense pressure. On July 30, 2011, Nektarina published a post announcing that my show was cancelled, stating that they supported my right to free expression and objected to the intimidation tactics by the Canadian embassy.

That was not the end of the story. I realized I needed to get hard evidence to expose the government censorship I was facing. So, I called up my friends Richard Littlemore and Brendan DeMelle at DeSmogBlog and asked for advice on how to file access to information requests.

With their assistance, I submitted my first ATI request on August 11, 2011. I expected to get the documents within the legislated 30-day time frame. But nothing came. While I waited, I started

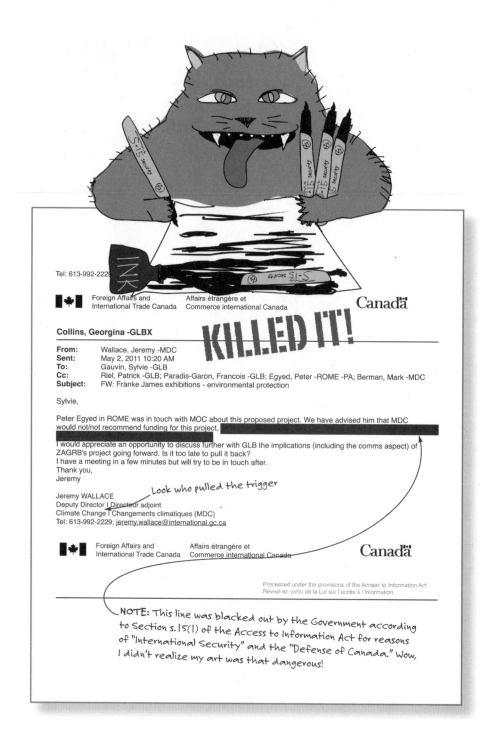

a crowdfunding campaign to mount a protest art show on bus shelters. By the end of the campaign, 82 people had contributed a total of $4,226. Wary of further interference by the government, I did not announce publicly where or when the show would take place.

Then in late October, a stroke of good fortune—I got word that the first release of ATI documents was ready. I travelled by train from Toronto to Ottawa to pick up the package from DFAIT on Halloween day. The timing sent shivers down my spine. Unbeknownst to them, my protest art show was set to open around the corner from the Parliament buildings on November 2. Those ATI documents were just what I needed to meet the press, and hold the government accountable. Those initial 165 documents were in fact gold.

Amy Chung obtained the ATI documents at the same time. She was not pleased to have been misled by the government in July. Chung wrote a follow-up article, "Government officials killed funding for Canadian artist: documents," on November 2:

> ... newly released documents obtained under access-to-information legislation show that Department of Foreign Affairs officials did initially earmark funding for James' show, only to withdraw their support days later, citing, among their reasons, that it "would run counter to Canada's interest."

With the ATI documents, I finally had the hard proof I needed. In the release package was a letter dated April 29, 2011, from Sylvie Gauvin, at DFAIT's Planning, Advocacy and Innovation office, approving $5,000 from their "Advocacy Funds budget." But three days later, the funds were cancelled by DFAIT's Deputy Director of Climate Change, Jeremy Wallace. The fact that the Climate Change office cancelled the funds is both ironic and Orwellian. DFAIT's assertion that supporting my climate change art "would run counter to Canada's interest" is telling indeed.

This is where ATI documents are invaluable. They can provide the concrete evidence that will expose corruption and reveal the truth.

Otherwise, the media—and Canadians—might just believe the fabrications that government bureaucats are feeding them.

Over the course of the next two years, I submitted more ATI requests, widening my search to include more government departments. By March 2013, I had gathered 2,172 documents, all related to me, from four different government departments. Among those thousands of pages, this nugget—first sent to me by the Privy Council Office—jumped out:

> However, it was later pointed out by another division that the artist's work dealt mostly with climate change, and was advocating a message that was contrary to the government's policies on the subject. So, after consultation, it was determined that the Canadian government would not fund the project after all.
>
> Jean-Bruno Villeneuve,
> Spokesperson Foreign Affairs and International Trade Canada

I was being censored for "advocating a message that was contrary to the government's policies." This is deplorable and violates my right to free expression, which is protected under the Charter.

In fortuitous timing, my book *Banned on the Hill* was just about to be published. For the book launch in May 2013, I drew inspiration from Villeneuve's quote. I created a poster of the Parliament buildings dropped into the Alberta tar sands.

Thanks to a crowdfunding campaign on Indiegogo, the "Do Not Talk" poster went up on transit poster spots on the streets of Ottawa in May 2013. It then appeared in Halifax in September. In November 2013, the posters popped up in downtown Calgary—coinciding with the Conservative Party's national convention. The "Do Not Talk" poster also travelled to the US. It went up on a bus shelter near Capitol Hill in Washington, DC, as part of my *Oh No Canada!* exhibition that ran from October to December 2013.

In 2014, *Banned on the Hill* won Gold and Silver book awards in the US. In June 2014, the BC Civil Liberties Association presented

DO NOT TALK ABOUT CLIMATE CHANGE

"The artist's work dealt mostly with climate change, and was advocating a message that was contrary to the government's policies on the subject."

Jean-Bruno Villeneuve, Spokespersonrole
Foreign Affairs and International Trade Canada

Processed under the provisions of the Access to Information Act
Révisé en vertu de la Loi sur l'accès à l'information

IT IS AGAINST GOVERNMENT POLICY

BANNED ON THE HILL

A True Story about Dirty Oil and Government Censorship by Franke James
Get the book at www.amazon.com and www.frankejames.com

me with its Liberty Award for Excellence in the Arts in recognition of my campaign to raise awareness about government censorship. I even got an unexpected thank you from an MP in Ottawa:

> Thank you, Franke, for your art and your activism. Those of us fighting in Parliament against the government's auditing of environmental groups, its muzzling of federal scientists, its decimation of Canada's environmental laws have a remarkable and passionate ally in you.
>
> Murray Rankin, October 9, 2014

Then, just when I thought we could wrap this story up, more evidence surfaced. The Office of the Information Commissioner (OIC) had responded to my 2013 complaint by launching an investigation. Their focus was on the legitimacy of the redactions that DFAIT used on my file. In February 2015, Bang-o!, the OIC found that the government had misused high-level security clauses to hide embarrassing and partisan comments. Ian MacLeod at the *Ottawa Citizen* reported on it: "The new versions of the documents show that much of the official concern over funding James and promoting the European art tour was based on the polarizing politics of climate change. In one, a departmental trade official notes that a Canadian diplomat in Europe would not help promote the show because of 'the artist's views on the oilsands.'"

This is what I thought all along. But now I had proof that the government is not content with "just" censoring what we create and publish. It actually wants to impede and limit our thinking too. They are telling us "Do Not Think about Climate Change: Your views may be a threat to Canada's security." And that presents a whole new level of danger.

I contacted Kevin Walby, co-editor of this book and associate professor of Criminal Justice at The University of Winnipeg, for his thoughts on the OIC's investigation. Here's a portion of his response:

The findings show that exemption clauses are not strictly followed and instead are applied to material simply because it does not fit into Stephen Harper's vision of Canada ... There is blatant evidence here of trying to protect the vested interest that Harper's Conservatives have in the oilsands ... Here we have abuse of access to information process, we have censorship, we have tyrannical information management, and all of those things are an affront to the idea of democracy, transparency and accountability.

Which brings me to the inspiration for *Games Bureaucats Play*. Filing ATI requests, and poring over thousands of pages of ATI documents, opened my eyes to how bureaucats misbehave—and why there is a pressing need to reform Canadian access laws. There are so many areas for improvement, it's astonishing. It's like they've purposely designed the system to thwart citizens who want information. They wouldn't do that, would they?

Although *Games Bureaucats Play* are satirical, they also contain the kernels for improvements of the system. Thirty years ago, when the ATI laws were first written, Canada was an international leader—but we have since fallen far behind. Suzanne Legault, head of the OIC, spoke frankly on *CBC Radio* about the need to update and reform our access to information laws: "Canadians should be angry. It's really a fundamental democratic right in Canada [and] it's linked to freedom of expression." That was in February 2013. Her call for action and reform was repeated again in June 2014 as she tabled the latest OIC annual report. Legault said, "I continue to have serious concerns about the health of the system, and the resulting harm to Canadians' right of access ... The urgent need to update the *Act* cannot be ignored."

Ironically, in 2006 the Harper Conservatives campaigned on promises of openness and accountability. "A Conservative government will 'oblige public officials to create the records necessary to document their actions and decisions.'" Who—if not us—is going to hold the government accountable for their promise?

GAME #1

HOT POTATO

BUREAUCAT RULE: As soon as you get a controversial file, a "Hot Potato", get rid of it. ASAP! And whatever you do, never write anything down! You might get caught later (i.e., held responsible for your actions).

BureauCats are cunning!
In this internal government email we see how easy it is to avoid creating records by using phone calls and having face-to-face meetings. Critics have asked that the ATI laws be strengthened so all government decisions must be recorded in writing.

From: Ljubenko, Vlatka -ZAGRB
Sent: May 3, 2011 8:37 AM
To: Fairchild, David -ZAGRB -GR
Subject: FW: Funding request - Climate changes project

FYI. Can you come to my office when Peter calls me to hear what it was about..?

From: Egyed, Peter -ROME -PA
Sent: May 3, 2011 8:32 AM
To: Ljubenko, V1atka -ZAGRB
Subject: Re: Funding request - Climate changes project

Hi Vlatka.
I'll be in the office shortly, and will call you to discuss this matter.

I first discussed the matter with Enrica, and then called Jeremy Wallace of the Climate Change division in DFAIT (MDC) to seek advice. He was the one who contacted Sylvie, who then called me after speaking with him.

Bye for now.
Peter
Sent from my mobile device I Envoye de mon appareil de mobilite

From: Ljubenko, Vlatka -ZAGRB
To: Egyed, Peter -ROME -PA
Sent: Tue May 0308:10:422011
Subject: FW: Funding request - Climate changes project

Hi Peter.

what happened yesterday? What did you talk to Sylvie about?

Kind regards.
Vlatka

GAME TIPS

How to play Hot Potato with your
bureaucats and WIN!
• Take careful notes
• Record all phone calls (as
  journalists do)
• Send 'written reports' (emails)
  and CC key players

Are you a Hot Potato?

Contrary to what you may think, getting a phone call from a bureaucat
is not necessarily a good sign. It could be an indication that you're a "hot
potato". A bureaucat's burning desire is to leave no trail, hence the verbal
communication.

Here's my email to Tristan Landry (Director of DFAIT Media Relations)
confirming what he told me in a phone call. Bet he loved it!

March 5, 2013 (via email)

Dear Mr. Landry,

Thank you for your phone call of February 1st confirming that the background description in Jean-Bruno Villeneuve's emails was written by the Department of Foreign Affairs. It was good to have the opportunity to clear up that issue directly over the phone with you.

I am contacting you today in the hopes that you will be able to provide information on what events led up to your phone call to me on February 1st, and what records exist. Today, ATIP officer Charles Bedard has declined my request to look for relevant records. My request to him was twofold:

1. Tristan Landry, the Director of Media Relations contacted me by phone on February 1, 2013. We talked for 7 minutes. Considering this fact it seems reasonable to assume that some records exist -- either emails, phone calls or meetings which led to his phone call.

2. Thomas Marr exchanged emails with me on January 22, 2013, therefore I know there are emails which you are missing.

Mr. Bedard suggested I file a complaint with the Information Commissioner. However re: #1 that seems to be a waste of taxpayer dollars and unnecessary red tape -- when I can simply write to you directly and ask about your decision to call me on February 1st. Considering Paul Brunet's January 11th email, it is logical to assume that your decision to call me was done in agreement with others. (Please see the pages from the ATIP document A-2012-02946 I C89 attached and emails below.)

I am also concerned at Mr. Bedard's unwillingness to 'retask' Mr. Marr. I have an email exchange with Mr. Marr which he could have provided, but chose not to. This is troubling as it points to a larger 'transparency' issue:

- Are there other Marr emails and records which have been withheld?

- Are there other DFAIT records which have been withheld?

I look forward to your reply by email or phone. Thank you.

Regards,

Franke

March 5, 2013 letter from Franke James to Tristan Landry, Director of Media Relations, Department of Foreign Affairs and International Trade.

GAME #2

SIT-ON-IT

BUREAUCAT RULE: Stall, delay, postpone. Do nothing. That's your job! Whenever anyone asks, tell them that they will have to wait until you are finished "doing your business".

GAME TIPS

How to outmaneuver the stalling bureaucat:
- File OIC complaints
- Write OIC commissioner
- Publicize the delay

"Meeting the original timeframe would unreasonably interfere with the operations of this department." That claim is standard bureaucat language. The kind you'll probably encounter in response to filing any Access request.

Are lengthy time extensions a clever ploy to torture you?

Well, not necessarily... It's just the bureaucats way of protecting their masters in Ottawa. The longer they can keep you from getting the information, the better the chances are that your news will be stale and irrelevant by the time you get your hands on it.

My complaints to the Office of the Information Commissioner (OIC) regarding time extensions have resulted in this acknowledgment, "We will record your complaint as well-founded"; but there is no penalty for delay.

The Canadian Journalists for Free Expression (CJFE) believes that for the "delays in the Access system to be significantly reduced, the powers of the Information Commissioner should be transformed from those of an ombudsman to those of an order-making tribunal."

In 2011 and 2012, I submitted complaints to the OIC about redactions and missing documents. Despite repeated follow ups, the files were caught in limbo. On April 4, 2013, I wrote to Suzanne Legault, the Head of the OIC, asking her to investigate...

Dear Ms. Legault,

I am very pleased to see that you are investigating the complaint regarding the muzzling of Federal scientists which was submitted by the University of Victoria Law Clinic and Democracy Watch.

My case is related to the government's muzzling of free speech, however I am not a federal employee. I am a Canadian citizen, an independent artist and environmental author, whose right to freedom of expression has been interfered with by the Federal Government.

I am writing to request that you investigate my complaints which were submitted in December 2011 and April 2012.

My story has been in the news many times since 2011, appearing in the Toronto Star, the Vancouver Sun, La Presse, the Vancouver Observer, and discussed on CBC radio's The Current, among others. Just recently my dilemma was featured in the *Freedom to Read 2013* magazine. I was honoured that Charles Montpetit, the freedom of expression coordinator at UNEQ, chose to shine a bright light on my case. Please see the article...

> *Return of the Blacklist* by Charles Montpetit (pages 18-19)
> Freedom to Read 2013: pdf link (or read it on my site)

The reason I was censored should make all Canadians angry—because it threatens the very essence of democracy: our right to speak up and disagree with our elected government.

Since August 2011, I have obtained over 2,000 pages of government documents through access to information laws. Many pages are redacted for reasons of "international security" and conversations with a Minister, but some reveal the startling truth as to why they interfered behind-the-scenes. In an internal government email, **Jean-Bruno Villeneuve**, government spokesperson at Foreign Affairs and International Trade Canada explains, *"the artists' work dealt mostly with climate change, and was advocating a message that was contrary to the government's policies on the subject."* (ATIP document: A-2012-02002_2012)

I am deeply concerned and frustrated by the delays on my complaints. As you know, "access delayed is access denied" and unfortunately, as the time drags on, my options on recourse become more and more limited. **I face the loss of my economic rights and legal remedies.**

I have spoken with Eric Murphy several times as to the delays. His explanation was that the redactions under section 15(1) and 21(1)(a) and 21(1)(b), require a specialized investigator.

My story will be in the news again very soon. I am publishing a new book which includes seven of my environmental essays from 2008-2013. It will also include a new essay on freedom of speech called, "Franke James is your fault?"

That perplexing title comes from an email letter written by the Canadian Embassy Trade Commissioner, Thomas Marr (see attached). As you can imagine, reading that subject line and seeing the heavily redacted letter was a shock to me—and is still distressing. I think the average Canadian would agree that Mr. Marr's letter is disturbing. And yet it is only one example of how the Federal government secretly interfered in my art show in Europe—causing its cancellation and the loss of a major business opportunity for me.

I hope that you agree that my case is urgent and should be investigated now.

Regards,

Franke James

April 4, 2013 letter from Franke James to Suzanne Legault, Head, Office of the Information Commissioner.

SUCCESS!

On April 10, 2013, the OIC responded to my email saying that they will investigate.

DOGGED DETERMINATION!

Although my initial conversations with OIC investigators suggested that my request would be resolved quickly, it took almost two years before I got a response. The case is not closed yet...

GAME #3

C.Y.A.

BUREAUCAT RULE: Always Cover Your Ass. And that means covering your boss's too, C.Y.B.A. Because if your boss—or worse your boss's boss—gets in trouble, your ass is out the door. So if someone wrote something down that might be embarrassing, cover it up! Redact it! It's a National (and job) Security issue!

Sometimes the Ottawa masters, and their sneaky little bureaucats, slip up. They accidentally write down the truth. That's when the black markers come out to censor whatever they foolishly put in writing.

Art about climate change? That must be labelled a dangerous threat to international security and dirty oil, S.15(1) International. If a Minister was involved that could be blacked out under section 21(1)(a) or 21(1)(b). I'd wager that embarrassment to the government is a major reason discussions about my art were blacked out!

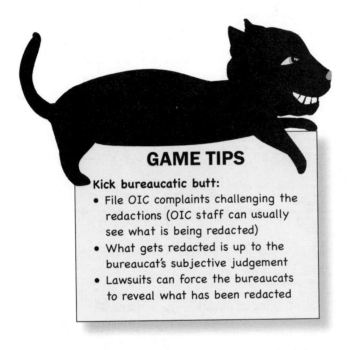

GAME TIPS

Kick bureaucatic butt:
- File OIC complaints challenging the redactions (OIC staff can usually see what is being redacted)
- What gets redacted is up to the bureaucat's subjective judgement
- Lawsuits can force the bureaucats to reveal what has been redacted

The Curious Case of the Disappearing Redactions

Take a look at the two letters on the next two pages. The letter on the left has white redactions. The same letter on the right has grey redactions. When I challenged Environment Canada (EC) that making redactions 'disappear' wasn't fair, they re-did them. They're so much easier to see in grey. Why would EC redact with white? (This correspondence, which DFAIT sent to EC, took one year and multiple complaints to obtain.) They appeared reluctant to admit the two departments talk to one another.

Can you spot the redactions in this letter?

Page 1 of 5

Paradis-Caron, Francois -GLB

From:	Wallace, Jeremy -MDC
Sent:	May 4, 2011 12:37 PM
To:	Gauvin, Sylvie -GLB
Cc:	Fairchild, David -ZAGRB -GR
Subject:	RE: Franke James exhibitions - environmental protection
Attachments:	FS$ FINAL.pdf

Sylvie,
I just had a useful discussion with David and had the opportunity to expand on the concerns related to the below. As I understand it. ZAGRB HOM would appreciate receiving a bit more background on the issue, which I am happy to provide.
Further to what I provided to David on our call just now, the following could be shared with ZAGRB HOM, if deemed helpful:

• funding has been provided to support climate-change related projects abroad to assist countries (in particular the most vulnerable) adapt to climate change;
• funding has also been targeted to facilitate other countries' substantive participation in international climate change negotiations within the UNFCCC;
• to my knowledge, we have focussed our funding at strengthening local capacity in other countries, and not/not towards Canadian speakers making presentations abroad on the subject of climate change;
As general guidance we would want to ensure that climate-change related support provided through departmental funds, while helping to address the challenge of climate change in tangible ways –in particular in those countries most vulnerable to its effects, (including Small Island Developing States);

MDC had concerns that the funding proposed below would not be consistent with our interests and approach outlined above, and would in fact run counter to Canada's interests more broadly, so we indicated to GLB that we would recommend against supporting.
Finally, while the funding Canada has provided within the context of Fast-Start Climate Financing, is of a different order of magnitude, I am enclosing for reference the 2-pager that was issued last fall, announcing the details of our $400 million contribution in 2010-11.
I hope this is helpful.
Jeremy

Jeremy WALLACE
Deputy Director | Directeur adjoint
Climate Change | Changements climatiques (MDC)
Tel: 613-992-2229; jeremy.wallace@international.gc.ca

s.15(1)

 Foreign Affairs and   Affaires étrangères et
International Trade Canada Commerce international Canada   Canadä

From: Wallace, Jeremy -MDC
Sent: May 2, 2011 10:20 AM
To: Gauvin, Sylvie -GLB
Cc: Riel, Patrick -GLB; Paradis-Caron, Francois -GLB; Egyed, Peter -ROME -PA; Berman, Mark -MDC
Subject: FW: Franke James exhibitions - environmental protection

Sylvie,
Peter Egyed in ROME was in touch with MDC about this proposed project. We have advised him that MDC would not/not recommend funding for this project,.

I would appreciate an opportunity to discuss further with GLB the implications (including the comms aspect) of ZAGRB's project going forward. Is it too late to pull it back?
I have a meeting in a few minutes but will try to be in touch after.
Thank you,
Jeremy

s.15(1)

Jeremy WALLACE
Deputy Director | Directeur adjoint
Climate Change | Changements climatiques (MDC)
Tel: 613-992-2229; jeremy.wallace@international.gc.ca

Foreign Affairs and   Affaires étrangères et
International Trade Canada Commerce international Canada   Canadä

This is the same letter, with redactions in grey.

Page 1 of 5

Paradis-Caron, Francois -GLB

From:	Wallace, Jeremy -MDC
Sent:	May 4, 2011 12:37 PM
To:	Gauvin, Sylvie -GLB
Cc:	Fairchild, David -ZAGRB -GR
Subject:	RE: Franke James exhibitions - environmental protection

Attachments: FS$ FINAL.pdf

Sylvie,
I just had a useful discussion with David and had the opportunity to expand on the concerns related to the below. As I understand it. ZAGRB HOM would appreciate receiving a bit more background on the issue, which I am happy to provide.
Further to what I provided to David on our call just now, the following could be shared with ZAGRB HOM, if deemed helpful:

• funding has been provided to support climate-change related projects abroad to assist countries (in particular the most vulnerable) adapt to climate change;
• funding has also been targeted to facilitate other countries' substantive participation in international climate change negotiations within the UNFCCC,
• to my knowledge, we have focussed our funding at strengthening local capacity in other countries, and not/not towards Canadian speakers making presentations abroad on the subject of climate change;
As general guidance we would want to ensure that climate-change related support provided through departmental funds, while helping to address the challenge of climate change in tangible ways –in particular in those countries most vulnerable to its effects (including Small Island Developing States)

MDC had concerns that the funding proposed below would not be consistent with our interests and approach outlined above, and would in fact run counter to Canada's interests more broadly, so we indicated to GLB that we would recommend against supporting.
Finally, while the funding Canada has provided within the context of Fast-Start Climate Financing, is of a different order of magnitude, I am enclosing for reference the 2-pager that was issued last fall, announcing the details of our $400 million contribution in 2010-11.
I hope this is helpful.
Jeremy

Jeremy WALLACE
Deputy Director | Directeur adjoint
Climate Change | Changements climatiques (MDC)
Tel: 613-992-2229; jeremy.wallace@international.gc.ca

s.15(1)

■✦■ Foreign Affairs and   Affaires étrangères et
      International Trade Canada   Commerce international Canada   Canadä

From: Wallace, Jeremy -MDC
Sent: May 2, 2011 10:20 AM
To: Gauvin, Sylvie -GLB
Cc: Riel, Patrick -GLB; Paradis-Caron, Francois -GLB; Egyed, Peter -ROME -PA; Berman, Mark -MDC
Subject: FW: Franke James exhibitions - environmental protection

Sylvie,
Peter Egyed in ROME was in touch with MDC about this proposed project. We have advised him that MDC would not/not recommend funding for this project,

I would appreciate an opportunity to discuss further with GLB the implications (including the comms aspect) of ZAGRB's project going forward. Is it too late to pull it back?
I have a meeting in a few minutes but will try to be in touch after.
Thank you,
Jeremy

s.15(1)

Jeremy WALLACE
Deputy Director | Directeur adjoint
Climate Change | Changements climatiques (MDC)
Tel: 613-992-2229; jeremy.wallace@international.gc.ca

■✦■ Foreign Affairs and   Affaires étrangères et
      International Trade Canada   Commerce international Canada   Canadä

GAME #4

STUPID CAT TRICKS

BUREAUCAT RULE: Information is dangerous! Especially in the wrong hands. If you must release any data to the enemy (citizens) make sure it's unsearchable, unshareable, and almost useless.

Dumb information? What's that? It's information that has been put through the Canadian government's access to information process. Federal bureaucats are busy taking our digital information and throwing it back to the 20th century—before computers were even invented.

Making our information "dumb" is laborious work and takes lots of taxpayer-funded time. The bureaucats start by taking government records (which may include emails, pin-to-pin messages, spreadsheets, diagrams, drawings, maps, reports, etc.), and they convert them into "scanned images" which they will send to you in response to an access to information request. You may get a thick stack of paper—or if you're smart enough to insist on it—electronic copies on a DVD, but it will all be "dumb" information, i.e., non-searchable and low-resolution.

Why do the Bureaucats do this? It makes it so hard to share, to search, and to analyze.

Fortunately there's an easy workaround for text. After accumulating hundreds of ATI documents I realized I needed a better way to search and analyze their contents than doing it manually. The answer of course is OCR software (Optical Character Reading software, like Adobe Acrobat). It changes the scanned images into searchable text. And it makes analyzing and fact-checking the documents so much easier. For example, there are 757 instances of "climate" in a 943-page ATI document I received. In those same 943-pages, my full name was mentioned 1,273 times. While Jeremy Wallace—the bureaucat who cancelled funding for my show because it ran "counter to government interests"—was mentioned 99 times. The OCR software makes it a breeze to post the information on the web—as searchable text.

But even though the information is searchable now—it's still all mixed up. The bureaucats are not focused on keeping citizens happy. They don't organize the documents chronologically, they just put them in the order they get them from various departments. To help you unravel it, it's worthwhile to create a table of contents. This will aid you in understanding the

GAME TIPS

Win the Information War!
- Request digital files or scan the ATI docs
- Use OCR software
- Post searchable data

content, reconstructing days—and seeing what is missing from the access documents. This analysis will be useful in filing a complaint.

GAME #5

GUILTY OR NOT

BUREAUCAT RULE: If you're searching for incriminating evidence, go ask the suspects!

I recall laughing out loud when my ATI bureaucat told me that they go directly to the "persons of interest" (A.K.A. "the suspects") and ask them to hand over the evidence. I asked him how their system made sense—'Why wouldn't the guilty just delete the incriminating files?'

My bureaucat responded with shocked alarm. There are "stiff penalties if anyone is caught doing that!" However, bureaucats are encouraged to delete "transitory" files (if it's prior to an access request being filed). So the message for bureaucats is simple: "delete early and often!" (See Game #6)

Not surprisingly some records are "missed" and are only obtained through others, e.g. "honest" bureaucats.

MOUSE? I DON'T SEE A MOUSE...

GAME TIPS

Get the evidence
- If the suspect's emails are only coming via 3rd parties, file complaints!

GAME #6

LITTER BOX BLOW-OUT!

BUREAUCAT RULE: Never leave anything in your litter box. So when in doubt, delete! After all, if the information doesn't exist, they can't use it against you.

TRANSITORY RECORDS

All employees must regularly delete transitory records.

Records Management and You! – an IM self-study module
Office of the Information Commissioner of Canada: www.oic-ci.gc.ca

TRANSITORY RECORDS AND ATI

"It is unlawful to delete any transitory record (email or document), once a formal ATI or Privacy request is received or anticipated by the Department, relating to the subject."

Records Management and You! – an IM self-study module
Office of the Information Commissioner of Canada: www.oic-ci.gc.ca

VOLUME AND ATIP ARE KEY ISSUES

• If kept, transitory records, and not just official records, must be provided under Access to Information and Privacy requests.

Records Management and You! – an IM self-study module
Office of the Information Commissioner of Canada: www.oic-ci.gc.ca

VOLUME AND ATIP ARE KEY ISSUES

• Transitory records are more likely to contain embarrassing !! and personal information.

Records Management and You! – an IM self-study module
Office of the Information Commissioner of Canada: www.oic-ci.gc.ca

Translation? DELETE FAST!

GAME TIPS

Get all the Dirt!
• Make ATI requests ASAP
• Track email chains and complain to OIC about missing emails/messages

Conflicting Messages?
Well yes. "Must regularly delete" versus "It is unlawful to delete". Oh dear! What's your Bureaucat going to do?

GAME #7

SPIES & PROWLERS

BUREAUCAT RULE: Every bureaucat must take an oath pledging loyalty to the government. Your duty is to monitor, track and snitch! Troll Twitter, Facebook and the line at the coffee shop.

Lilkoff, Marie~Christine -BCM

From: Driscoll, Lynne -BCM
Sent: June 14, 2012 1:50 PM
To: *BCM Spokespeople / *BCM Porte-parole
Cc: Brown, Debora -BCD
Subject: Franke James -Twitter

This is what Chris pulled together for us this morning. Note that the media monitoring report is top of the list ......

Franke James

Franko_Forward Jun 13, 8:23pm via Buffer
RT @Bergg69 "(DFAIT) media monitoring report from July 2011 lists James as "an inconvenient artist" ("une artiste qui dérange"), t... bit.ly/LViPig

plrstweet 9:04am via Tweet Button
@frankejames: Canadian Embassy representative in Croatia, the commissioner Thomas Marr asks: "Franke James is your fault?"   is.gd/x3P3U1 #cndpoli

frankejames Jun 13, 9:41pm via Tweet Button
Canadian Embassy representative in Croatia, the commissioner Thomas Marr asks: "Franke James is your fault?" is.gd/x3P3U1 #cndpoli

Elizabeth May Jun 13, 8:30pm via Twitter for BlckBerry®
@etenbrislux I have been working with Franke James and trying to uncover the blacklisting by govt. #cdnpoli #c38

e
RT @blairp   gd/SZR4eG

b
A disgrace!   SZR4eG

Right of Freedom of Expression:
Article 19 of the Universal Declaration of Human Rights: "Everyone has the right to freedom of opinion and expression; this right includes freedom to hold opinions without interference and to seek, receive and impart information and ideas through any media and regardless of frontiers".

GAME TIPS

Playing with Prowlers:
- File ATIs to monitor and track the trackers
- Use social media as a public forum to express your ideas
- Speak out! The Canadian Charter protects Free Expression

Pogue, Lisa -TRNTO -TO

From:	Feir, Jim -TRNT
Sent:	July 28, 2011
To:	Pogue, Lisa -T
Cc:	Rice, Candice -TRNTO -TO; Rauth, Sue -TRNTO -TO; Vogtle, Janice -TRNTO -SSO -TO
Subject:	FW: **Foreign Affairs Hot Issues** I Questions importantes des affaires étrangères : 28.07.2011
Importance:	High
Follow Up Flag:	Follow up
Flag Status:	Green

Lisa - please note the article near the end of this dealing with the same matter as Candice's forwarded message of last night.

Let's discuss this am when you get in.

Thanks, Jim.

From: Media Analysis / Analyse Medias (BCM)
Sent: July 28, 2011 6:55 AM
Subject: Foreign Affairs Hot Issues / Questions importantes des affaires étran

Foreign Affairs Hot Issues / Questions importantes des affaires é

-FOREIGN POLICY I POLITIQUE ÉTRANGÈRE:

LIBYA: As Libya settles into stalemate, the West looks for a way o

LIBYA: Sinking deeper into a quagmire in Libya (VicTC A10, Barry

AFGHANISTAN: Suicide bomber kills populist Kandahar mayor (StJ

WAR CRIMINALS: Fourth 'war criminal' arrested (KWR A3)

SOMALIA/TERRORISM: Terror recruiter target Somali-Canadian Women (Edj A14)

ARCTIC SOVEREIGNTY: Don't stop believing (The Economist)

INDIA / PAKISTAN: The fresh face of Pakistan finds favour with India (VSUN B

SERBIE / KOSOVO : Des Serbes attaquent des soldats de l'OTAN (JdM 28 et

-CORPORATE ISSUES I QUESTIONS CORPORATIVES:

ARTS / FRANKE JAMES: Une artiste qui dérange (LAP A6)

TABLEAUX: Ottawa devrait les expédier à Québec, dit le PQ (TRI 10 et autres)

-EVENING BROADCAST NEWS HEADLINES I BULLETINS DE NOUVELLES NA

01/11/2011

GAME #8

PEEK-A-BOO!

BUREAUCAT RULE: As an instrument of the government, every bureaucat has secret agent super-powers! Use these powers to track citizens and keep on eye on everything they do, just in case...

To play the bureaucats' Peek-A-Boo game you'll want to decode their identities and their acronyms. By understanding who is looking at your file you can gain valuable insight into the behind-the-scenes power dynamics—and who is really pulling the strings.

The bureaucats who are directly involved in email conversations will be easy to spot (they will usually have their titles in their emails). But who are all the other bureaucats and Federal departments copied on the correspondence? To find out, two online tools will help you break the code. Take the "cc" list and drill down using GEDS, the Government Electronic Directory Services. (Note that not all departments list their employees so you may need to use a more robust online search tool like Google.)

GAME TIPS

Out-spying the spies!

- Use govt sites and Google to identify the watchers and decode acronyms
- Create a spreadsheet to list people, departments, and related documents

---

The eyes on the following page are an example of just some of the hundreds of bureaucats who are monitoring my file. Knowing that senior bureaucats, such as the *Director of the Cabinet Relations Division*, the *Head of the Energy Secretariat*, and the *Cabinet and Parliamentary Affairs Division*, are watching shows how far up the food chain my case has gone—and gives me insight into what may be under the redactions.

The bureaucats also use nonsensical acronyms that make it tricky for outsiders to understand what's going on. For example Foreign Affairs' "Climate Change and Energy Division" is dubbed "GDC". The initials "DCL" reveal that the bureaucat is with the "Cabinet and Parliamentary Affairs Division", while the innocuous "C5" at the end of an email address indicates that the bureaucat has an email on DFAIT's "secret" email system. Many Federal departments list their acronyms and symbols, so breaking their codewords just requires a little diligence and online searching.

Arvelin, Leonard -DCP -C5

From:	Arvelin, Leonard -DCP -C5
Sent:	December 8, 2011 1:50 PM
To:	Van Essen, Talina -MINA -C5; EXTOTT (MINA C5); EXTOTT (MINT C5)
Cc:	Fry, Robert -DCD -GR -C5; Belmahdi, Latifa -BCF -C5; Blais, Sylvie -DCL -C5; Daigle, Johanne -DCP -C5; Landriault, Maureen -DMT -C5; Chenard, Andrée -DCD -C5; Pomel, Simon -USS -C5; Tremblay, Philippe -MINA -C5; McCulloch, Monique -DCP -C5; Vienneau, Helen -DCP -C5; O'Donnell, Pamela -IRC -C5; Petit, Pierrette -BCD -C5; Popesco, Tatiana -MINT -C5; Petrisor, Corinne -MINT -C5; Mueller, Mike -MINT -C5; Wheeler, Stewart -BCF -C5; EXTOTT (BCF C5); EXTOTT (CMR C5); EXTOTT (CSM C5); EXTOTT (DCL C5); EXTOTT (DMA C5); EXTOTT (DMT C5); EXTOTT (GGD C5); EXTOTT (JLD C5); EXTOTT (MINA C5); EXTOTT (USS C5); EXTOTT (CMC C5); Lau, Meghan -MINA -C5; Mackey, Timothy -MINA -C5; IM Repository / Répertoire de GI; Cole, Emily -DCP -C5
Subject:	COMM Alert -MINA - Access to Information Act - A-2011-00802 / LA: All communications regarding Art Show and/or artist Franke James, from March 2011 to present (August 16, 2011).

Security/Sécurité: SECRET / SECRET

You have expressed an interest in seeing the release package related to the following Access to Information request:

Ms. Sylvie Blais, Cabinet and Parliamentary Affairs Division, Parliamentary Affairs Officer, Foreign Affairs and International Trade Canada: Blais, Sylvie -DCL -C5;

Mr. Simon Pomel, Deputy Director, Foreign Affairs and International Trade Canada: Pomel, Simon -USS -C5;

Mr. Mike Mueller, Director of Parliamentary Affairs, Public Safety Canada: Mueller, Mike -MINT -C5;

Mr. Gary Pringle, Head, Energy Secretariat, Foreign Affairs and International Trade Canada, Energy Secretariat: Pringle, Gary -MDCE

Mr. Robert Fry, Director General and Corporate Secretary, Foreign Affairs and International Trade Canada, Corporate Secretariat: Fry, Robert -DCD -GR -C5;

Mr. Stewart Wheeler, Director, DFAIT, Cabinet Relations Division: Wheeler, Stewart -BCF -C5;

Mr. Andre-Marc Lanteigne, Director General - Communications, Foreign Affairs and International Trade Canada: Lanteigne, Andre-Marc -CSM

Ms. Latifa Belmahdi, Director BCF, DFAIT, Foreign Policy and Corporate Communications: Belmahdi, Latifa -BCF -C5;

GAME #9

HALOS OR HORNS?

BUREAUCAT RULE: All bureaucats follow a strict code of honesty and never tell any lies unless it is necessary to protect the nation's security, their leader's integrity, or open up a career opportunity.

How do you catch a bureaucat telling a lie? As George Orwell wrote in 1946, "Political language is designed to make lies sound truthful and murder respectable, and to give an appearance of solidity to pure wind." Before you make any public accusations, you'll need hard evidence—that's where ATI documents can help.

"POLITICAL LANGUAGE IS DESIGNED TO MAKE LIES SOUND TRUTHFUL & MURDER RESPECTABLE, & TO GIVE AN APPEARANCE OF SOLIDITY TO PURE WIND"
George ORWELL / 46

The ATI documents I've received since 2011, show that the bureaucats were making 'misleading' statements to the media. Below is an example of an internal backgrounder which directly contradicts the government's public statements.

Internal Backgrounder:

"Canadian artist Franke James* had originally asked several Canadian embassies in Europe for funding for her art tour in Europe. Most declined the offer, except for the embassy in Zaghreb, which, after consultation with GLB, had initially agreed to provide the funding.

"However, it was later pointed out by another division that the artists' work dealt mostly with climate change, and was advocating a message that was contrary to the government's policies on the subject. So, after consultation, it was determined that the Canadian government would not fund the project after all."

Jean-Bruno Villeneuve
Spokesperson, Foreign Affairs and
International Trade Canada

Public Statements:

"Funding was never withdrawn, nor was it guaranteed."

"Ms. James' characterisation of her dealings with Canadian officials does not appear to be based on facts."

"It is not the Department's practice to interfere with private sponsorships of Canadian artists abroad."

Jean-Bruno Villeneuve
Spokesperson, Foreign Affairs and
International Trade Canada

GAME TIPS

Getting the truth...
- Use ATIPs to compare public statements with internal conversations

---

* *Actually Nektarina contacted the Canadian Embassies for funding.*

GAME #10

THE BLAME GAME

BUREAUCAT RULE: When all else fails—you're caught with the hot potato, it's in writing, and denials don't work, then do the dishonourable thing... Blame it all on someone else.

Thomas Marr is a Trade Commissioner at the Canadian Embassy in Berlin. He used to be the Ambassador to Croatia (where this story all started). This is how he knew Vlatka at the Canadian Embassy in Croatia. Marr wrote to Vlatka asking her if I was her "Fault".

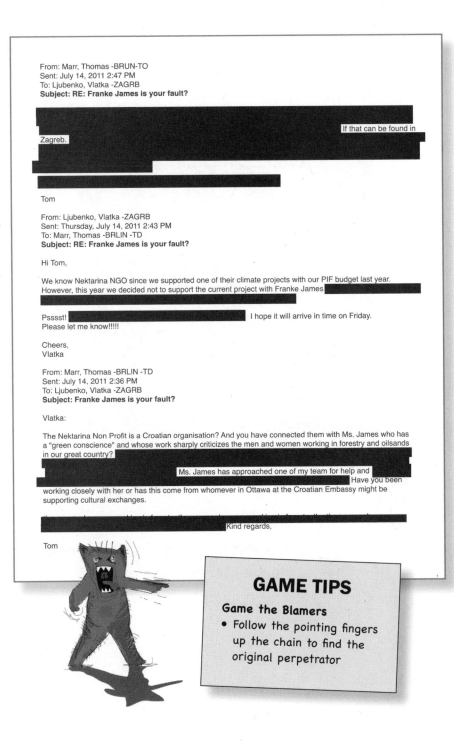

From: Marr, Thomas -BRUN-TO
Sent: July 14, 2011 2:47 PM
To: Ljubenko, Vlatka -ZAGRB
Subject: RE: Franke James is your fault?

██ If that can be found in
Zagreb. ███████████████████

████████████████████████████████

Tom

From: Ljubenko, Vlatka -ZAGRB
Sent: Thursday, July 14, 2011 2:43 PM
To: Marr, Thomas -BRLIN -TD
Subject: RE: Franke James is your fault?

Hi Tom,

We know Nektarina NGO since we supported one of their climate projects with our PIF budget last year.
However, this year we decided not to support the current project with Franke James ████████████

Psssst! ████████████████████████ I hope it will arrive in time on Friday.
Please let me know!!!!!

Cheers,
Vlatka

From: Marr, Thomas -BRLIN -TD
Sent: July 14, 2011 2:36 PM
To: Ljubenko, Vlatka -ZAGRB
Subject: Franke James is your fault?

Vlatka:

The Nektarina Non Profit is a Croatian organisation? And you have connected them with Ms. James who has
a "green conscience" and whose work sharply criticizes the men and women working in forestry and oilsands
in our great country? ████████████████████████████
████████████████ Ms. James has approached one of my team for help and
██ Have you been
working closely with her or has this come from whomever in Ottawa at the Croatian Embassy might be
supporting cultural exchanges.

██
████████████████████████████ Kind regards,

Tom

GAME TIPS

Game the Blamers
- Follow the pointing fingers
  up the chain to find the
  original perpetrator

And the Government said,

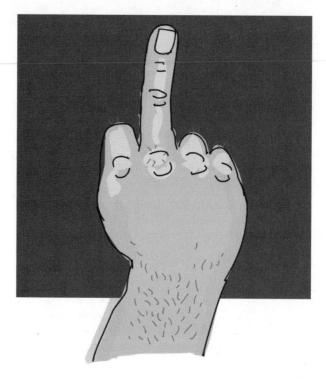

"I don't believe it is our responsibility to address the Charter claims Ms. James is making."

Jean-Bruno Villeneuve,
Spokesperson | Porte-parole
Foreign Affairs and International Trade Canada

Winning the Game

How can you win against bureaucats who are playing devious games with you? Here are three strategies that can help improve your odds of winning.

I. Alert the Referee

The bureaucats will continue to play dirty unless we call them out. Unlike sporting games, the "referee" (the Office of the Information Commissioner or OIC) is not even watching the game. So it won't call penalties unless we lodge a complaint. Then the referee is obligated by law to look and see whether our complaint is well founded. If it is, they will investigate matters and seek an appropriate resolution. (Note that federal cuts to the OIC's budget have reduced the number of investigations they can do each year.) The OIC's "notable investigations" provide useful summaries of cases the Commissioner has investigated annually.

2. Go Public

Most Canadians trust the bureaucats to do their jobs honourably. So when their underhanded tactics are exposed to the Canadian public (a.k.a. the voters) it is a shock that shakes our faith in our elected government, and democracy itself. Gather your ATI evidence and then seek out national and international media who will share your news with the public. Consider launching a publicity campaign on TV, radio, outdoor media, and social media to spread the word of their misdeeds. Crowdfunding makes this type of mass media campaign possible—and it's very democratic.

3. Be Transparent

The bureaucats are breaking the rules and getting away with it. Our strongest weapon to hold them accountable is a tool they hate: transparency. So use it! Digitize and post your ATI documents. Don't forget to make them searchable and use keywords (so Google and other search engines can find them). The bureaucats will continue to play obstruction games. That's why we need to work together to make updating and strengthening ATI laws a priority. Good luck in your access to information pursuit—and have fun beating the bureaucats.

Because Our Voices Joined Together Have the POWER to CHANGE GOVERNMENTS.

CHAPTER 6

PEEKING BEHIND THE CURTAIN: ACCESSING THE BACKSTAGE OF SECURITY INTELLIGENCE THREAT ASSEMBLY

Alex Luscombe and Michael-Anthony Lutfy

The high level of official secrecy that security intelligence agencies claim to require makes them a special kind of "public service." Leaks, memoirs, and whistle-blowers aside, as lay outsiders most of what we know about security intelligence is based on what security experts tell us in the form of media statements and public warnings about potential threats. In this chapter, we consider federal access to information (ATI) law as a means to better understand the inside work of security intelligence organizations in Canada. The analysis of internal ATI-generated records puts us as researchers in a unique position to address the question of how security experts assemble information about alleged threats to national security. By "assembly" we mean the amalgamation of disparate knowledge forms (e.g., psychological profiling, statistical probabilities, agent field notes) to generate an argument that an individual or group poses a security threat.

Using ATI we gain partial and mediated access to the "backstage" of threat assembly. Specifically, we investigate the backstage work of threat assembly using insider records produced through ATI on three intelligence agencies: the Canadian Security Intelligence Service (CSIS), the Royal Canadian Mounted Police (RCMP), and the Financial Transactions and Reports Analysis Centre of Canada (FINTRAC). Our chapter has two main parts. First, we review previous research on security intelligence threat assembly, focusing on what it means to analyze a backstage intelligence report collected through ATI. Second, we distinguish and analyze three strategies of threat assembly in Canadian intelligence work: conflation, ontological brainstorming, and "monkey see, monkey do." We argue that understanding security intelligence work in terms of these three strategies is useful for academic research, social activism, and journalism. We conclude by considering some additional implications of using backstage texts to research government security and intelligence threat assembly.

Security Intelligence Threat Assembly

The authority of intelligence agencies is defined by their ability to access secret sources of information, to know things that we, as ordinary citizens, cannot. The expert knowledge of intelligence agents is secret and, according to this line of reasoning, necessarily so. As Peter Gill and Mark Phythian (2006: 7) put it:

> A lack of secrecy endangers the comparative advantage sought from the intelligence. If a target is aware that information is being collected on it, that knowledge could impact on the process by allowing the target to feed (dis)information into it, or adopt other counter-measures.

This argument is popular in scholarly and journalistic work on intelligence and is the core rationale for secrecy articulated by intelligence officials themselves. But there is more to secrecy than strategic or tactical advantage. Gill and Phythian (2006:7) suggest that secrecy is also about the protection of intelligence work from public scrutiny:

> Secrecy also raises key issues of legality, morality and accountability. It creates an unchallengeable political space for its customers, because they base their actions on *supposedly superior analysis*. Because this is secret, it is denied to others and so cannot easily be challenged (emphasis added).

Simply put, secrecy protects intelligence work from outside inspection, which affords intelligence agents greater scope and flexibility in the ways they assemble expert "knowledge."

We propose that another way to assess the relationship between secrecy and intelligence work is to view secrecy as a constitutive element of expert claims about what or who is a national security danger. According to this view, secrecy is not an "add-on" to security intelligence work (as if secrecy and security intelligence were independent of one another) but part of what makes it possible in the first place. Without secrecy, at least some of the decisions made by intelligence agencies (e.g., arrests, imprisonments, deportations, etc.) would be confronted and challenged. Blanket secrecy, unless challenged through methods such as ATI or the courts, means that virtually every intelligence-based decision is deemed just and legitimate.

If security intelligence takes place backstage, most citizens have little sense of what security experts are doing when they inform us of new national security concerns. For example, CSIS offers the following front stage declaration on the section of its website called "The Threat Environment": "Domestic extremists in Canada are capable of orchestrating acts of serious violence" (Government of Canada 2014). Implicit in this threat declaration is the assumption that security agents know something about "domestic extremists" that we, the public, cannot. But is this always the case?

Analysis of backstage texts from ATI has made us skeptical. In fact, it is doubtful that intelligence work as a whole is much different than other political or bureaucratic work. As Eva Horn (2011: 119) argues:

> The best kept secret of modern intelligence agencies is their mundane daily routine: the protracted, often tedious collection of data from frequently tarnished sources, the laborious checking and evaluating of information, and the tricky diplomatic art of communicating to the government the political and military knowledge obtained.

The bureaucratic work of intelligence agencies may serve some useful purposes, but maximizing the efficiency of information flows
and generating innovative thinking are not among them. The added
elements of heightened secrecy, task compartmentalization, political bias, and "groupthink" in intelligence bureaucracies only work
to further hinder these processes. In short, intelligence expertise is
far from perfect, but it can certainly *look* perfect when all we read
are the carefully assembled press releases of media relations officers.

The broader point is that intelligence work, often presented as
seamlessly rational and scientific on the front stage (objective threat
"identification"), is in reality inefficient and subjective. This is what
we mean when we use the term threat "assembly," which captures
the messy and ambiguous character of intelligence work in the backstage. The process of identification presupposes certain inherent or
objective criteria against which a threat is being compared. However,
often these criteria surface only after the threat has been assembled.
Below, we build on these points by analyzing internal security intelligence documents collected through ATI with an eye to concep-
tualizing different strategies of threat assembly.

Typology of Security Intelligence Threat Assembly

Conflation

The strategy of conflation involves pairing unlike cases based on
minor and insufficient similarity, culminating in a new understanding of one or more of these cases. Jeffrey Monaghan and Kevin Walby
(2012) used ATI to expose CSIS's use of "Multi-Issue Extremism," a
category employed by CSIS to group Indigenous activists, animal
rights activists, and other generally non-violent social movement
groups into a single threat assemblage. The Multi-Issue Extremism
category stems from CSIS's drive to make investigable those political
groups that do not otherwise fit within their mandate to monitor
threats to Canadian national security by labelling them as ideological

"extremists," and therefore potential terrorists. By permitting access
to the primary intelligence reports that develop such concepts, ATI
allows us to get at the root of "threat claims" by revealing elements
of the internal reasoning and arguments behind them (in this case
the careful conflation of terms grounded in a crude generalization
about a group's ideological tendencies or propensity for violence).

Another example of conflation can be found in a backstage CSIS
report on the antiglobalization movement. The report conflates
learning your rights as a legal subject with a social movement tactic or counter-strategy:

> Anti-globalization protesters employ a variety of tactics....
> Nonetheless, it is clear that certain violent actions on the part of the
> militant protesters are illegal and constitute a threat to public safety
> ... [redacted] Participants [redacted] and are usually found at the
> forefront of protests employing radical direct action tactics, includ-
> ing property damage and civil disobedience, which often leads to
> violence ... *Anti-globalization activists also incorporate post-
> demonstration tactics by preparing for arrests, interrogations,
> and trial. They gain awareness of their rights in the event of arrest
> or detention and write telephone numbers for free legal aid arrest
> centres on their arms* (request #1463-02/11-09, emphasis added).

Along with talk of threats to public safety and property damage
comes the mention of awareness of legal rights and access to lawyers, as if the latter were somehow a violent and nefarious protest
tactic to be reasonably grouped in and conflated with the others.
The acquisition of legal knowledge is recast as an indicator of threat.

Conflation is also evident in the RCMP Intelligence Assessment
Report on the Freemen on the Land (FOTL) movement (shared with
CSIS's Integrated Threat Assessment Centre and included in request
#A-2012-400). The report defines the FOTL as "a sovereign citizens'
movement consisting of unorganized groups or persons claiming
to have severed all ties with the government of Canada." Here the

notion of "sovereign citizen" is used as an umbrella category to group together anyone who rejects the authority of the state or government, and the FOTL is considered alongside individuals and groups that do not necessarily self-identify as Freemen but act violently. In this way, the FOTL is the recipient of a network spillover effect; it is reframed as potentially or increasingly violent through association. As the report states:

> In the United States, there are numerous examples of sovereign citizens who have embraced politically-motivated violence, notably Oklahoma bomber Terry Nichols in April 1995 and Scott Roeder, who killed an abortion doctor in Wichita, Kansas in May 2009 ... The Federal Bureau of Investigation (FBI) considers sovereign citizens' movements among the top domestic terrorist threats to the US, along with animal rights / eco-terrorism, anarchists and lone offenders with extremist agendas ... Interaction with Sovereign Citizens from the United States, who tend to gravitate to more violent means, may influence Canadian FOTL proponents to a higher level and frequency of violence than what has been seen to date.

Through the conflation of "sovereign citizens" and the FOTL, properties and characteristics that did not exist prior to the threat assembly process are added to the FOTL profile. The origin of these properties (i.e., conflation) can be forgotten once the label of "threat" has been achieved. Our point is not to suggest that the FOTL are innocent or deserving of immunity from intelligence agents (given recently reported incidents involving the group, we believe there is cause for concern). What we question is the means, or the argumentative strategy through which the FOTL are branded as dangerous. In this case, the strategy is conflation.

A final example, again from our research on the Freemen movement, is the category of "paper terrorism," by which the RCMP means:

> Activities initiated through the legal system intended to bog down institutions through the time and effort required to address them

... FOTL often send these, often long-winded, letters to law enforcement, government departments and agencies ... The letters
are attempts to have authority figures recognize, or at least address, assertions made by FOTL proponents. Paper terrorism includes activities where individuals forward ... often nonsensical,
documentation.[1]

While the RCMP intelligence report invokes Kafkaesque imagery of
a despondent bureaucrat buried in mounds of paper, there is every
reason to question the concept of "paper terrorism." To perpetuate
the use of this concept, either the definition of "spamming" is being
raised to an act of violence against bureaucracy (which assumes that
bureaucracy is something that could be the victim of violence) or the
definition of "terrorism" is being expanded to include non-violent
forms of dissent. ATI provides a glimpse into precisely what activities the FOTL are engaged in that garner the label of "paper terrorism," and in turn we are able to judge for ourselves whether or not
to accept this label. Paper terrorism, as defined by the RCMP, is not
a concept we would hear in press statements or annual reports (not
yet, anyway). It is instead a concept that forms the backstage of
government decision-making, presently accessible only through ATI.

Ontological Brainstorming

ATI teaches us that moments of "public threat declaration" are frequently preceded by a series of backstage meetings over the question
of "how"; that is, how a person, group, organization, or object is a
threat in need of government intervention. We refer to these internal meetings as "brainstorming" sessions. When people brainstorm,
they tend to keep an open mind and consider possibilities that may
or may not be feasible. This is frequently what intelligence agents
do when they discuss possible ways to redefine the nature, meaning,
or intentions (the ontology) of a person, group, or thing. In this way,
intelligence agencies are, intentionally or not, (re)defining ontologies. Brainstorming sessions typically begin from the proposition

"x equals threat," but there may be no legitimate explanation as to why (in some cases, as noted below, it is simply because the US has said so). Through brainstorming, intelligence agents quite literally make a threat of something: the reasons that "x" is a threat come to life.

Intelligence threat assembly is not just about the behaviours of people, but also the material and virtual objects that surround them (Aradau 2010; Neyland 2009). David Neyland (2009) has analyzed how everyday objects, such as letters, scissors, and garbage bags, can be recast as threats. He shows how objects can have different meanings and identities to different people in particular contexts. For example, the everyday ontology of scissors-as-paper-cutting-device can easily be replaced by an ontology of threat, scissors-as-weapons, in airport security lineups where scissors are prohibited as carry-on items. From this literature we draw the insight that brainstorming sessions are often discussions about the redefinition of object ontologies. Debates over object ontologies seldom take place in public. The organizations we are interested in—security intelligence agencies—tend to have minimal interest in collaborating with researchers, and are in many ways barred from doing so under Canada's *Security of Information Act*. ATI is one possible way to access intelligence agencies' brainstorming.

Consider the case of Bitcoin, a new digital currency created in 2008. Bitcoin markets itself as an open-source, innovative, and easy-to-use means of digital transaction. The Financial Transactions and Reports Analysis Centre of Canada, however, has a very different image of the new currency. Under the mandate of FINTRAC, transactions over $10,000 have been recast as suspicious, and the private sector must report all transactions equal to or greater than $10,000 to FINTRAC. A similar process of ontological redefinition has occurred with the emergence of new currencies. As FINTRAC states in its public report on money laundering and terrorism: "According to investigators, an emerging digital currency named 'Bitcoin'... could also be a method used by criminals to make anonymous international transactions" (Government of Canada 2011). But how did FINTRAC arrive at this statement? Here we consider a recent internal discussion led by a FINTRAC "[redacted s.17] Developer Extraordinaire" and "[redacted s.17] Analyst" on the rising popularity of Bitcoin in Canada.[2] This otherwise secret conversation is available in the form of an internal PowerPoint presentation released through ATI (request #A-2013-00019).

To begin, the title of this presentation, "Digital Currencies: Why Should FINTRAC Care?," is misleading, or at least poorly phrased. To ask the question of why FINTRAC should care about digital currencies such as Bitcoin would seem to suggest a neat and tidy list of reasons or *a priori* properties that directly implicate Bitcoin within FINTRAC's broadening lens of concern. In other words, the "why" question presumes a threat identification process. But the presentation does not go on to provide evidence of a threat, and surely there is nothing inherently suspicious about an alternative currency. A more accurate title would be "Digital Currencies: *How* should FINTRAC care?" because the presentation is really an exercise in ontological brainstorming.

The possibilities brainstormed by FINTRAC are diverse. One strategy is to portray Bitcoin as irregular by comparing it with other "private currencies" in order to raise concern about Bitcoin's "lack of limitations." Examples include (i) Bitcoin/Airmiles: "Airmiles are not convertible into cash or negotiable outside that business," (ii) Bitcoin/Disney dollars: "Disney dollars can be used by local businesses but are not currency beyond a particular precinct," and (iii) Bitcoin/tribal currencies: "African tribes often have currencies only accepted within that tribe." According to this line of reasoning, exchange limitations are construed as regular or normal, thus raising alarm bells about the increasing ease through which Bitcoin can be swapped for other currencies such as cash. There is also discussion of the users of Bitcoin: "Regulars allegedly [include] cybercriminals, identity thieves, online fraudsters and child pornographers." By referring to this diverse assemblage of dangerous regulars, FINTRAC has at its disposal a rich toolkit of practical and discursive possibilities for threat assembly. By uniting Bitcoin with child pornography, for example, FINTRAC can invoke a moral imperative to regulate. There are even claims about energy use: it is estimated "that in just 24 hours, [Bitcoin] miners used about $147,000 of electricity just to run their hardware"; "That is 982 megawatt hours a day, enough energy to run 31,000 homes." Other points of interest include the anonymity of Bitcoin users: "What are they going to report? Computerguy101 sent money to Computergirl102?" Anonymity, according to FINTRAC, allows for an absence of a "central authority": "No one to set limitations and to regulate"; "Libertarians and Drug Dealers do not want to have to report to 'the man.'" The threat of hackers is also cited: "Hackers motivated to reduce confidence by shutting down exchanges in hopes that they may buy low." Finally, there are assertions about Bitcoin's unlawful foundations: "Main followers used to be: computer geeks, drug-dealers and libertarians"; "Silk Road (black market underground website) is what made Bitcoin so popular to begin with."

As a new intelligence agency, FINTRAC began by reframing all transactions valued at $10,000 or more as a potential threat. This threat assembly strategy was later extended into the realm of monetary transactions generally, assembling the notion of the "suspicious transaction" on the grounds that suspicious individuals were beginning to collapse large transactions into many smaller ones to elude the $10,000 threshold. The current direction of FINTRAC's brainstorming sessions suggests quite a different approach to threat assembly. The agency is no longer simply focusing on specific transactions, but on the use of alternative currencies as a key threat. Such a blanket approach to threat assembly raises significant concerns for social activists and others who are experimenting with alternative currency forms.

Brainstorming is an example of how an individual or group identity, or an object's ontology, can be changed and shaped under the auspice of suspicion, behind closed doors. ATI allows us to view how these agencies define which threats are "real" and which are not, expose internal justifications for government intervention, and predict state responses to new ontologies.

Monkey See, Monkey Do

ATI is useful for researching the practices of single intelligence agencies, but also the relations between intelligence agencies in networks. Research on social networks demonstrates that networks of individuals, groups, and organizations (called "nodes") are rarely, if ever, characterized by equality (Kadushin 2012). For security and intelligence scholar Didier Bigo (2006), conflict in intelligence networks is the norm, with each agency holding different views over what should and should not be seen as a threat. As intelligence experts have become more integrated in the post-9/11 period, certain agencies have risen to prominence within intelligence networks. In transnational networks especially, US agencies typically act as models and reference points. Not surprisingly, US nodes hold particular prominence in Canada given our status as a "junior partner" in the "Five Eyes" intelligence network made up of the US, UK, New Zealand, Australia, and Canada. Canada faces intense pressure to do its part and cooperate with US interests. The Delisle leaks are a case in point. Following the intelligence leaks by Canadian naval officer Sub-Lieutenant Jeffrey Delisle to Russian intelligence authorities in 2013, Canada was warned by the US and other members of Five Eyes that if information retention protocols were not improved, Canada would no longer be considered a trustworthy partner (Chase and Taber 2013).

In many of the backstage intelligence reports we analyzed, US security agencies are cited as sources of evidence and as impetus for threat assembly, sometimes with little or no elaboration. Although this project is a work in progress, we call this monkey see, monkey do. As noted in the RCMP intelligence report on the FOTL discussed above: "The Federal Bureau of Investigation (FBI) considers sovereign citizens' movements among the top domestic terrorist threats to the US, along with animal rights / eco-terrorism, anarchists and lone offenders with extremist agendas." By invoking reference to the FBI, the RCMP (and by extension, CSIS, which is at the receiving end of the report) is able to further legitimize its claims about Freemen as a "policing and security concern." Bigo (2002: 74-75) suggests that the "ethos of secrecy and confidentiality" that defines intelligence culture creates within the profession a "community of mutual recognition" that reproduces "a logic of implicit acceptance of claims made by other professionals." Certainly, there is a transnational community of mutual recognition evident in the backstage records on Canadian Freemen. Of the fourteen intelligence reports listed under "Appendix A —Resources reviewed," four are from the FBI and one is from the Washington Regional Threat and Analysis Center. Threat assembly in one geopolitical context (the US) is referenced to back claims about threat in another (Canada), as if the two nations—and, by extension, the groups under investigation—were one and the same.

We came across another example of monkey see, monkey do in the FINTRAC PowerPoint presentation on Bitcoin, which included a slide titled "Relevance to FINTRAC?" This slide offers a summary list of six reasons why FINTRAC might care. One of them states that the threat assembly of Bitcoin is relevant because "Our partners are recognizing it," in particular the US Financial Crimes Enforcement Network (FinCEN), a reflection of FinCEN's continuing leadership role in the broader financial intelligence community (Beare and Schneider 2007). According to the speaker, "FinCEN has stated that it is not illegal and has released an Official Guidance regarding the use of Digital Currencies." The point is not necessarily how FinCEN has opted to assemble the situation, deeming digital currencies legal but regulated, but simply that *they have* taken action against the currency, providing FINTRAC with a strong impetus to follow suit. While in some cases there may be acceptable reasons to follow the actions of another node in an intelligence network, it can be dangerous as a general strategy. In this particular report the actions of FinCEN, an intelligence agency in another country with its own socio-economic conditions and problems, are cited as if they had a direct bearing on those in Canada, but with little critical comparison or nuance. We cannot simply assume that the use of alternative currencies in one jurisdiction is identical to their use in another. In the social sciences, scholars are regularly chastised for making similar leaps of faith (e.g., Doob and Webster 2006). It should also be noted that the FINTRAC intelligence initiative itself is a product of US pressure. During the 1990s, Canada refused to construct an intelligence agency independent from existing organizations like CSIS. But with mounting political pressure from the US and the US-steered Financial Action Task Force, Canada eventually agreed to pass a new federal anti-money laundering bill, later amended to include terrorist financing, which led to construction of FINTRAC in 2000 (Beare and Schneider 2007).

Intelligence records we have accessed reveal several instances where the US security intelligence juggernaut acts as both an expert source of authority and an impetus for threat identification. When cited as an authority, the claims of US agencies are often uncritically accepted. Referring to the findings of other intelligence agencies gives their claims a kind of universal significance and applicability outside of the localized context in which they were produced. Canadian threats to national security are labelled as such by virtue of the actions and assessments of their imagined counterparts in other jurisdictions, often with little to no concern for the Canadian context. By the time the results of threat assessment are presented to the Canadian public, identifying "*x*" as a threat to national security, we are unlikely to be informed of its basis in non-Canadian intelligence practices. While it is customary in all forms of knowledge communication to cite experts, the role of Canadian agencies as experts comes into question if they are blindly deferring to a foreign authority.

Conclusion: The Hidden Assembly of Circular Truths

Mainstream discourses on intelligence emphasize the power of political decision-making informed by expert assessment of information gleaned from secret sources. The sources remain secret for their protection and the results, in the form of intelligence reports and other documents, are kept away from the hands of the "enemy" (and therefore the public) in the name of comparative advantage. By opening the backstage of intelligence work, ATI shows that intelligence agencies are as involved in threat assembly as they are in threat identification, and that threat assembly is an act of knowledge creation.

Using assembly as a method of knowledge creation is popular in all research, from social science research to security intelligence, and it does not necessarily make something "less true" simply because it was the product of assembly. That being said, much of the so-called expert knowledge produced by intelligence agencies through threat assembly is highly suspect. Security intelligence agencies routinely feed us truths about threat in our country, truths that the public is expected to accept at face value. We are expected to trust, accept, and not ask questions about intelligence-based decisions. ATI is important because it allows us to question the circular logic of bureaucratic truths and bring contentious files front and centre for public viewing.

While we accept that not all threat assembly reports can be publicly accessible, more ought to be. The use of ATI to this end is not "anti-intelligence," it simply helps to bring intelligence threat assembly more in line with the values of critical journalism and academia by holding them to a higher standard of production. It also emboldens the public's right to know about important security decisions that are being made in its name. As Horn (2003: 66) argues, "Whereas the crowning achievement of scholarly research is publication, which opens the possibility for contradiction, intelligence is blind. It is created, circulated, and eventually discarded in an imaginary space" that is closed to the public. The categories of conflation, ontological brainstorming, and monkey see, monkey do can help us make sense of the threat assembly processes we encounter in internal documents released through ATI, and help to yield a more democratically engaged assessment of what, who, or why something becomes a national security matter.

NOTES

1   The RCMP categorizes these letters as follows:

- A "Claim of Right" is a document drafted by FOTL proponents to identify themselves to authorities. These documents generally claim a right to refuse the authority of lawful officials or institutions, to possess and use firearms or explosives in the defense of their beliefs, property or families, or to possess and produce illegal drugs.
- "Notice of Increase in Mandate" is a document presented by FOTL adherents to an official to provide the authority to comply with demands, usually economic, made by the FOTL. FOTL proponents believe that, through their sovereign nature, they have the ability to delegate financial authority as they see fit.
- The "Notice to Act as Teller" is a document that is provided to the Bank of Canada indicating a FOTL follower wishes to assume the ability to withdraw government funds for their personal use.

2   Section 17 of the *Access to Information Act* states: "The head of a government institution may refuse to disclose any record requested under this Act that contains information the disclosure of which could reasonably be expected to threaten the safety of individuals."

REFERENCES

Aradau, C. 2010. Security that Matters: Critical Infrastructure and Objects of Protection. *Security Dialogue* 41(5): 491-514.

Beare, M. E. and S. Schneider. 2007. *Money laundering in Canada: Chasing Dirty and Dangerous Dollars.* Toronto: University of Toronto Press.

Bigo, D. 2006. Globalized (In)Security: The Field and the Ban-Opticon. In D. Bigo and A. Tsoukala (eds.), *Illiberal Practices of Liberal Regimes: The (In)Security Games.* Paris: L'Harmattan.

_____. 2002. Security and Immigration: Toward a Critique of the Governmentality of Unease. *Alternatives* 27(1): 63-92.

Chase, S. and J. Taber. 2013. Convicted Spy Delisle Sold CSIS Names to Russians, Court Told. *The Globe and Mail,* January 31.

Doob, A. and C. Webster. 2006. Countering Punitiveness: Understanding Stability in Canada's Imprisonment Rate. *Law & Society Review* 40(2): 325-368.

Gill, P. and M. Phythian. 2006. *Intelligence in an Insecure World.* Malden, MA: Polity.

Government of Canada. 2014. *Domestic and Multi-Issue Extremism.* At <csis-scrs.gc.ca/ththrtnvrnmnt/trrrsm/dmstcnmltssxtrmsm-en.php>

_____. 2011. Money Laundering and Terrorist Activity Financing Watch: April-June 2011. At <fintrac-canafe.gc.ca/publications/watch-re-gard/2011-10-eng.asp>

Horn, E. 2011. Logics of Political Secrecy. *Theory, Culture & Society* 28(7-8): 103-122.

_____. 2003. Knowing the Enemy: The Epistemology of Secret Intelligence. *Grey Room* (11): 59-85.

Kadushin, C. 2012. *Understanding Social Networks: Theories, Concepts, and Findings.* New York: Oxford University Press.

Monaghan, J. and K. Walby. 2012. Making Up 'Terror Identities': Security Intelligence, Canada's Integrated Threat Assessment Centre and Social Movement Suppression. *Policing and Society* 22(2): 133-151.

Neyland, D. 2009. Mundane Terror and the Threat of Everyday Objects. In K. F. Aas, H. O. Gundhus, and H. M. Lomell (eds.), *Technologies of InSecurity: The Surveillance of Everyday Life.* New York: Routledge-Cavendish.

ACCESS TO INFORMATION REQUESTS

SIRC request #1463-02/11-09

CSIS request #A-2012-400

FINTRAC request #A-2013-00094

CHAPTER 7

ATI/FOI RECORDS AND PRISON EXPANSION IN CANADA:
HOW TO GET THE WORD OUT

Justin Piché

If electoral politics is like a body of water into which one casts stones to cause ripples to control the political agenda and impress voters, throwing enough stones toward the opposing shoreline may create a wave that will force foes to retreat inland. When it comes to recent political debates on penality in Canada, it is safe to say that successive federal Conservative governments under Prime Minister Stephen Harper have made getting "tough on crime" one of their central planks since 2006. From their shoreline they have thrown stones of criminalization and punishment at an unprecedented pace, sending their political opponents running far from the water.

As noted elsewhere (Mallea 2011; Moore and Donahue 2008; Piché 2013), the Conservatives have unleashed dozens of new laws and policy reforms to this end. First and foremost, they have introduced sentencing measures in a stated effort to send more of the convicted to prison (e.g., reductions in the number of offences eligible for conditional sentences or house arrest), for longer terms of incarceration (e.g., the creation of new mandatory minimum sentences), with fewer opportunities for prisoners to be released into the community prior to completing their sentences (e.g., the elimination of accelerated parole review). They have implemented administrative procedures designed to make federal penitentiaries less inhabitable for prisoners (e.g., removing incentive pay for prison labour). Measures have also been put in place in the name of "public safety" that often frustrate efforts by the criminalized to reintegrate into their communities after having done their time (e.g., further eligibility restrictions on applying for and receiving a pardon).

While much of the literature on access to information (ATI) and freedom of information (FOI) is oriented toward promoting the usefulness of ATI/FOI requests as a data production technique (e.g., Walby and Larsen 2012), the challenges encountered during the information brokering process (e.g., McKie 2012), and the need for legal action and legislative reform to enhance state transparency (e.g., OIC 2013; Yeager 2006), this chapter focuses on how to make data obtained through ATI/FOI more accessible to the public. More specifically, I discuss how I mobilized information about prison capacity expansion in Canada by drawing on newsmaking criminology approaches (Barak 1988). Following Henry (1994), I argue that these approaches are well-suited to disrupt hegemonic discourses concerning "crime" and "justice" circulating in the news and entertainment media that reinforce punitive ways of thinking about criminalized harm. I show how messages organized around the deployment of ATI/FOI records, which are valued as credible information sources in media and political circles, were useful in providing opponents of the Conservative agenda with stones to cause their own political ripples. This altered, at least for a time, the way political debates on penality were fought in Canada.

Obtaining ATI/FOI Data

The Conservatives have often refused to disclose projections of the costs and consequences of their "law and order" agenda. For example, during House of Commons and Senate proceedings concerning the *Truth in Sentencing Act* (2009) that imposed stringent limits on credit given for time served to individuals awaiting trials and sentencing hearings behind bars, then Liberal Public Safety critic Mark Holland (2009) turned to the Parliamentary Budget Office of Canada (PBO) to examine its implications. He did so because, in his words, the "government has supplied Parliament with no costing for these policies, despite the fact that the cost to our correctional system will inevitably be in the hundreds of millions of dollars as a significant influx of new federal inmates will result." During this period, I wondered how many new prison spaces were going to be built to accommodate the expected influx of new prisoners in federal penitentiaries operated by Correctional Service Canada (CSC), which incarcerate people serving sentences of at least two years plus a day. I also wanted to know what prison expansions were planned in provincial-territorial facilities mandated to incarcerate individuals awaiting bail determination, trial, and sentencing, as well as people serving sentences of up to two years less a day.

In searching for information on the scope of new penal infrastructure in early 2009, I discovered that the public information available online was insufficient (Piché 2012). So, I turned to other means of generating the data. With a background in filing ATI and FOI requests to obtain unpublished information on the warehousing of security certificate detainees (Larsen and Piché 2009) and tours of CSC facilities (Piché and Walby 2010), I decided that this could be a fruitful way to unearth these new state secrets on prison expansion.

To lay the groundwork for my ATI/FOI requests, I compiled what online information I could and began to request information over the phone from federal employees (and their provincial-territorial counterparts) about prison capacity expansion initiatives (see Piché 2012). I incorporated this initial information (e.g., the location of planned projects) into my ATI/FOI requests to reduce the likelihood that recipients would deny the existence of the initiatives I was investigating. Although I encountered numerous barriers in my ATI/FOI research, such as outrageous fee estimates and time delays, by February 2010 I had unearthed close to 40 penal infrastructure projects totalling 6,000 additional prisoner beds and $3 billion in construction-related costs at the provincial-territorial level alone (Piché 2012). In contrast, had I relied on publicly available information, I would have only been able to identify eleven of these projects.

More importantly, I would not have arrived at the surprising conclusion that most of these new facilities and expansions to existing prisons were not being developed in response to federal penal reforms. Rather, they were being erected to account for a massive surge in the number of legally innocent individuals awaiting judicial proceedings behind bars over the past few decades (Deshman and Myers 2014; Piché 2014). The federal government only disclosed its $600 million prison capacity expansion plan in June 2010—which took the form of over 2,700 new prisoner beds in dozens of new units on the grounds of existing penitentiaries and increases in the use of double-bunking—after pressure from journalists, parliamentarians, and the Parliamentary Budget Office of Canada (Head 2010; Piché 2011).

Publicizing ATI/FOI Data

In electoral politics, there are matters that political parties consider to be "sword issues." These are policy areas that they believe themselves to be credible in, and that can be used to attack their adversaries to generate political support. In contrast, "shield issues" are policy areas that parties believe they are less credible in, and therefore need to go on the defensive, or find a way to change the channel, when such matters are raised. While these battle metaphors may seem more appropriate for World of Warcraft enthusiasts than for elected representatives, they are precisely the terms used by the federal Conservatives to describe the current political terrain (see Wingrove 2013).

"Crime and punishment" is an obvious example of what the Conservatives consider to be a sword issue. This is illustrated by remarks made by Ian Brodie, Harper's former chief of staff, during a talk he gave at the McGill Institute for the Study of Canada's 2009 annual conference. At the conference, Brodie noted that "sociologists, criminologists, and defence lawyers" who criticize their penal reforms are "all held in lower repute than Conservative politicians."

As a result, he said, "politically it helped us tremendously to be attacked by this coalition … we never really had to engage in the question of what the evidence actually shows about various approaches to crime" (Geddes 2009). As Brodie suggests, academic and legal critiques of harsher criminalization and punishment in Canada do not deter the Conservatives from engaging in their punitive agenda. Therefore, there was a need for other kinds of critiques that might force the Conservatives to raise their shields.

With a sizable amount of information about ongoing prison construction already in my possession (most of it collected using ATI/FOI requests in 2009), I thought it would be an opportune time to analyze the data in order to (i) craft digestible messages derived from my research findings (stones); (ii) identify targets (ponds) who exerted influence in debates about penal policy and practice; and (iii) communicate (cast) messages that might destabilize the claims-making terrain and allow for alternative narratives to circulate about prison expansion and incarceration. Making previously unpublished government records accessible, searching for collaborators and forums who give record-holders a platform to share their findings, and developing ways to keep information circulating beyond their initial exposure are all common challenges for ATI/FOI users. Drawing on newsmaking criminology, the remainder of the chapter discusses how I tackled each of these challenges in turn.

Carving Stones

With several hundred pages of government records, one approach to messaging and dissemination would have been to simply create an online archive of Canadian prison expansion files that activists, journalists, and researchers could freely access. The downside of this strategy is that the initial information generator loses an opportunity to draw connections and contextualize the materials, to target particular individuals and organizations who might best make use of them, and to strategically time their release to generate attention in ways that are contingent on novelty and unpredictable events. As noted by Roberts (2012: 117) in his critique of the "leak, publish, and wait for the inevitable outrage" strategy that WikiLeaks initially adopted, new information disclosures hardly guarantee an audience, or one that understands complex material. Whether obtained by leaks or by ATI/FOI users, unpublished government documents need to be analyzed. And messages derived from them need to be well crafted, because, in "its undigested form, information has no transformative power at all" (ibid.: 130). In my view, limiting information disclosures to their mere publication is a liberal project that is overly focused on reformism as opposed to more radical change (Curran and Gibson 2013).

Electing to maintain as much control as I could over the data and its analysis and dissemination, I initially focused on the justifications that governments offered for not disclosing records (see Piché 2012). From there, I identified key infrastructure project details (e.g., facility locations, number of additional prisoner beds, construction-related costs) and the bureaucratic justifications for building new prison spaces (see Piché 2014). Based on readings of state documents, which ranged from ministerial briefing notes about prison capacity to reports detailing why new infrastructure projects were needed, I carved out two key messages based on my ATI/FOI findings.

First, I amassed a paper trail showing that CSC and the federal government were consistently denying Canadians access to information concerning their prison construction plans. Not only did they refuse to disclose any records pertaining to prison expansion, but they went so far as to claim that no such plans existed (see Piché 2011). They continued to do so in spite of an article in CSC's *Let's Talk* magazine published a year earlier, which indicated that the government was in the process of deciding how it would "modernize" its prison infrastructure (Head 2008). This stood in sharp contrast to their provincial-territorial counterparts, who all disclosed—to a greater or lesser extent—information about their penal infrastructure initiatives. Thus, I was in a solid position to illustrate how the federal Conservative punishment agenda lacked transparency.

Second, in the wake of the 2008 economic crisis, when Canadians were being warned of the "tough choices" that would have to be made to balance the budget, I pointed to the billions of dollars being spent on new prison spaces. I also questioned what more Canadians could expect going forward in terms of prison building to accommodate the touted influx of new prisoners serving longer sentences, and what other sacrifices would need to be made in the context of "austerity" (see Piché 2015).

Having carved these two stones, I turned my attention to finding ponds to cast them into in a way that would maximize the ripples, and help keep information circulating about ongoing prison expansion in Canada. Here, I drew on key texts within the newsmaking criminology literature.

Finding Ponds

In preparing to disseminate my ATI/FOI findings, I crafted a list of key players that had been involved in recent penal reform debates in Canada. Chief among them were journalists and columnists working for prominent media outlets that covered federal politics (e.g., CBC News, CTV News, The Globe and Mail, National Post, Toronto Star, Sun News). I also searched for reporters who worked for smaller news outlets that had a history of covering prison issues (e.g., Kingston Whig-Standard).

These targets were privileged for two reasons. First, ATI/FOI records are an important and common source of data used in journalism. The documents I generated could provide me with access to these actors. Second, because the news media plays a central role in shaping political debates and public opinion on penality, engaging these members of the commentariat is key to challenging "prevailing structures of meaning [e.g., about imprisonment] and displacing these by new conceptions, distinctions, words and phrases, which convey alternative meaning" (Henry 1994: 289). These new ways of seeing and describing the world can be thought of as "replacement discourses" (ibid.).

While targeting members of the press can provide a conduit to disseminate ATI/FOI findings, this information can also shape subsequent media coverage of government policies and practices. In an effort to steer opponents of the Conservative punishment agenda to adopt some of the messages I had crafted, I compiled a list of federal parliamentarians sitting in opposition who were spokespersons for their respective parties on public safety and (in)justice issues in the House of Commons and the media. I also drafted a list of prominent advocates and non-profit organizations who worked in the punishment sector and who frequently participated in media debates on penal reform. With these targets identified, my objective was to disseminate messages based on my research findings to create a ripple effect beyond the initial splashes of information.

Casting Stones

Following the generation of information about prison construction in Canada and the identification of target audiences, I used several dissemination strategies to get the word out. Again, some of these tactics were informed by the literature on newsmaking criminology. These approaches allowed me to introduce discourses that—along with the efforts of others—helped to challenge the relative monopoly that the Conservatives (and their "tough on crime" agenda) had in recent debates on Canadian penality.

One approach to newsmaking criminology I adopted was self-reporting as the subject of a news story (Henry 1994). This strategy involved organizing and participating in public forums and inviting journalists, and releasing findings directly to news outlets. The strength of this tactic is that it positions those who are releasing information as "the prime, if not exclusive source of the story," which circumvents the potential for "experts disagree" scenarios and allows for greater depth in terms of the messages one is able to communicate (p. 296). An example of this tactic is the public forum I organized in Ottawa on February 17, 2010, where I first publicized my findings about prison capacity expansion. After providing an overview of the scope, justifications, and costs of new penal infrastructure, I raised questions about the federal government's lack of transparency, including "what kind of penal expansion will we experience once the Correctional Service of Canada announces its 'major construction initiatives'?" I also asked several questions about the costs of these policies, such as "Do we really want to live in a country that constructs prisons ahead of schools, hospitals, and public transportation?" As noted elsewhere (Piché 2015), these two messages caught on in the media (see MacCharles 2010) and were mobilized, along with other initiatives that lacked cost transparency (e.g., the purchase of F-35 fighter jets), by the Liberals to bring down the minority Conservative government in a 2011 confidence motion.

A second approach to newsmaking criminology I used was journalistic work. During my doctoral work at Carleton University in Ottawa, I had the opportunity to write four op-ed pieces in the Canadian news media. Nevertheless, it was clear that gatekeeping practices at some media outlets prevented me from publishing certain stories. To circumvent this problem, I turned to blogging. I incorporated this do-it-yourself approach to journalism by using my blog—*Tracking the Politics of 'Crime' and Punishment in Canada*— to disseminate my findings. During my most active years as a blogger (2010 and 2011) I sent posts to journalists, columnists, parliamentarians, and non-profit executives who would often relay my lines of inquiry and ATI-generated information in their own communications.

Mobilizing my findings in these ways led to further opportunities to publicize my ATI/FOI research. I was invited to react to and comment on emerging news stories in various media outlets as a subject matter expert. By cultivating professional relationships with members of the press, as Greek (1994) recommends, I was also able to function as an "educative provocateur" by offering advice and directing my target audiences to relevant information that could be brought to bear on penal reform debates (Henry 1994).

One of the great advantages of ATI/FOI information is that it can often be employed in public policy discussions. For my part, I used information on prison capacity expansion to further ongoing debates about the need to develop alternative ways of thinking about criminalized harms. I drew on my research in briefs to the House of Commons and the Senate, as well as an unsolicited report to the Provincial-Territorial Heads of Corrections, which led to appearances before each of these bodies. Publicizing my ATI/FOI findings in these ways helped to prolong and widen discussions on the costs and lack of transparency of penal infrastructure expansion in Canada for years after the first wave of data I disseminated in February 2010.

Communication Matters

In this chapter, I have argued that the combination of ATI/FOI records and an approach to information dissemination informed by newsmaking criminology can provide activist researchers with tools for raising questions about state policies and communicating their research findings. For those interested in engaging in public policy debates—whether it be on criminalized harms and punishment or any other important topic—ATI/FOI records provide a credible base from which users can gain access to (and influence) members of the news media and others involved in the policy-making process. Using this data and these strategies, I managed to disseminate information about new penal infrastructure over the course of hundreds of media interviews, dozens of public presentations, and several non-scholarly works that generated public interest and policy change. State actors and other opponents can try to shoot the messenger, but the messages bolstered by ATI/FOI findings are not easily assailable. They are, after all, based on the state's own information. Above all, what this research taught me is that the communication networks developed through sharing and communicating ATI/FOI disclosures are critical to working toward social justice in Canada.

REFERENCES

Barak, G. 1988. Newsmaking Criminology: Reflections on Media, Intellectuals, and Crime. *Justice Quarterly* 5(4): 565-587.

Curran, G. and M. Gibson. 2013. WikiLeaks, Anarchism and Technologies of Dissent. *Antipode* 45(2): 294-314.

Deshman, A. and N. Myers. 2014. Set Up to Fail: Bail and the Revolving Door of Pre-trial Detention. Toronto: Canadian Civil Liberties Association.

Geddes, J. 2009. Ian Brodie Offers a Candid Case Study in Politics and Policy. *Macleans*, March 27.

Greek, C. E. 1994. Becoming a Media Criminologist: Is 'Newsmaking Criminology' Possible? In G. Barak (ed.), *Media, Process, and the Social Construction of Crime: Studies in Newsmaking Criminology.* New York: Garland Publishing.

Head, D. 2010. Prisons are Ready for the Rush. *Toronto Sun*, June 23.

_____. 2008. Modernization of Physical Infrastructure. *Let's Talk* 33(1): 13-15.

Henry, S. 1994. Newsmaking Criminology as Replacement Discourse. In G. Barak (ed.), *Media, Process, and the Social Construction of Crime: Studies in Newsmaking Criminology.* New York: Garland Publishing.

Holland, M. 2009. Letter to Mr. Kevin Page, Parliamentary Budget Officer. Ottawa, October 21.

Larsen, M. and J. Piché. 2009. Exceptional State, Pragmatic Bureaucracy, and Indefinite Detention: The Case of the Kingston Immigration Holding Centre. *Canadian Journal of Law and Society* 24(2): 203-229.

MacCharles, T. 2011. Provinces to Spend $2.7B on Prisons. *Toronto Star*, February 20.

Mallea, P. 2011. *Fearmonger: Will Stephen Harper's Billions for his Tough-on-Crime Agenda Make Our Streets Any Safer?* Toronto: Lorimer.

McKie, D. 2012. Access to Information: The Frustrations – and the Hope. In M. Larsen and K. Walby (eds.), *Brokering Access: Power, Politics, and Freedom of Information Process in Canada.* Vancouver: UBC Press.

Moore, D. and E. Donahue. 2008. Harper and Crime. In T. Healy (ed.), *The Harper Record.* Ottawa: Canadian Centre for Policy Alternatives.

Office of the Information Commissioner of Canada (OIC). 2013. Summary of Submissions: Open Dialogue on Modernizing the Access to Information Act. Ottawa. At <oic-ci.gc.ca/eng/summary-submissions-sommaire-soumission.aspx>

Piché, J. 2015. Playing the 'Treasury Card' to Contest Prison Expansion: Lessons from a Public Criminology Campaign. *Social Justice* 41(3): 145-167.

_____. 2014. A Contradictory and Finishing State: Explaining Recent Prison Capacity Expansion in Canada's Provinces and Territories. *Penal Field* xi.

_____. 2013. Le Régime de Sanctions de Harper. *Nouveaux Cahiers du Socialisme* 9: 119-125.

_____. 2012. Accessing the State of Imprisonment in Canada: Information Barriers and Negotiation Strategies. In M. Larsen and K. Walby (eds.), *Brokering Access: Power, Politics, and Freedom of Information Process in Canada.* Vancouver: UBC Press.

_____. 2011. 'Going Public': Accessing Data, Contesting Information Blockades. *Canadian Journal of Law and Society* 26(3): 635-643.

Piché, J. and K. Walby. 2010. Problematizing Carceral Tours. *British Journal of Criminology* 50(3): 570-581.

Roberts, A. 2012. WikiLeaks: The Illusion of Transparency. *International Review of Administrative Sciences* 78(1): 116-133.

Walby, K. and M. Larsen. 2012. Access to Information and Freedom of Information Requests: Neglected Means of Data Production in the Social Sciences. *Qualitative Inquiry* 18(1): 31-42.

Wingrove, J. 2013. Tories Facing Heat for Compiling 'Enemies' Lists for New Ministers. *The Globe and Mail*, July 16.

Yeager, M. 2006. The *Freedom of Information Act* as a Methodological Tool: Suing the Government for Data. *Canadian Journal of Criminology and Criminal Justice* 48(4): 499-521.

CHAPTER 8

BEYOND ATIP:
NEW METHODS FOR RESEARCHING STATE SURVEILLANCE PRACTICES

Christopher Parsons

Governments have long conducted surveillance of communications and communications systems. Whereas communications surveillance historically entailed the physical tapping of telephone cables, steaming of envelopes, or accessing telegraph cables, contemporary forms of communications surveillance involve the deployment of malware on desktops and network switches, the mass capture and collection of "metadata," and legal orders used to extract personal information from domestic telecommunications operators. The Citizen Lab, which is a multidisciplinary research laboratory at the Munk School of Global Affairs within the University of Toronto, has explored different aspects of such communications surveillance over the past decade. Since 2013, we have undertaken an extensive analysis of how Canadian government authorities access telecommunications data from Canadian Internet Service Providers (ISPs), such as Rogers Communications, Bell Canada, and TekSavvy Solutions. In the course of our research, we have used access to information requests that were directed towards federal, provincial, and municipal government agencies, alongside a series of novel research methods that have relied on public letters, personal information-requesting tools for citizens, dialogues and engagements with Members of Parliament, and routine discussions with journalists. In all cases, we used these techniques to elicit information about how, and why, government agencies gain access to Canadians' telecommunications information that is transited or stored by Canadian ISPs.

We adopted this range of research methods because contemporary surveillance techniques are mired in secrecy. Canada's federal government does not disclose statistics about telecommunications surveillance practices and, in some cases, assumes contradictory positions about whether companies can disclose the extent of their assistance to government agencies. The result is that researchers, citizens, academics, and journalists alike are left without a comprehensive or accurate understanding of what kinds of surveillance practices the government of Canada and Canadian corporations are undertaking, the regularity and legality of those undertakings, or even the legal rationales for the practices themselves.

This chapter focuses on the challenges of studying the difficult and often obscure issue of Canadian state and corporate surveillance. Researchers routinely turn to Access to Information and Privacy (ATIP) requests to cut through this obscurity, but the laws are often too weak, too poorly enforced, or too full of deliberate loopholes and blind spots to provide comprehensive awareness about surveillance. Thus, additional methodological techniques are needed to pierce the veil of government secrecy. But what kinds of techniques can be successful, what are their limitations, and how effective are they? How can researchers better understand the kinds of surveillance programs the federal government is conducting now, and has conducted in the past? I begin by discussing the merits and drawback of federal ATIP legislation, a legal tool that is routinely used to learn about the scope and dimensions of state surveillance. In light of the ATIP regime's relative limits in revealing the contours of federal surveillance, I discuss how researchers can use a variety of political, regulatory, and legal techniques to increase government accountability and corporate transparency. Importantly, the methodological proposals I assess have the effect of *adding to* as opposed to *replacing* data received under ATIP. By adopting an expanded set of methodological techniques, researchers can better fill out and make sense of the often limited revelations that emerge from the ATIP process.

The Benefits and Limitations of ATIP

Access to Information and Privacy laws are meant to facilitate processes of democratic governance by ensuring that citizens "have the information required to participate meaningfully in the democratic process, and secondly, that politicians and bureaucrats remain accountable to the citizenry."[1] The capacity to publicize otherwise non-public government decisions allows journalists, academics, and other motivated members of society to inform their fellow citizens about the actions of their governments (Birkinshaw 2006). When it comes to state surveillance practices in particular, ATIP laws are meant to provide much-needed insight into the operations of the state's security apparatus. Although complete openness of security and surveillance operations could compromise the state's ability to protect its citizens (Roberts 2005a), overzealous secrecy undermines citizens' abilities to understand, authorize, and reform proposed or existing state practices. ATIP and other right of access legislation is typically designed to strike a balance insofar as reviews of sensitive information are conducted so that released information does not undermine the state's ability to protect the population. However, this balance often means that states feverishly redact information. Therefore, we need to ask how Canadian ATIP laws can be used to understand existing state surveillance practices and, further, what their limitations are.

ATIP requests can take many forms. They can be historical in nature, broad in scope, or narrowly designed to access specific documents. Historical requests uncover or release information that has been previously disclosed to another person under ATIP legislation. In the United States, historical requests concerning governmental surveillance can involve downloading previously completed requests from freedom of information non-profit organizations (e.g., Muckrock.com). In contrast, historical requests in Canada require either requesting documents previously released under ATIP from public listings or, in the case of requests that are too old to be listed online, requesting a ledger of previously completed ATIP requests and filing a new request to access them.

Historical requests provide insights into the contours of proposed, ongoing, or since-terminated surveillance operations. At the Citizen Lab, we requested previously filled ATIPs from a range of federal agencies that were responsible for handling lawful access and telecommunications security portfolios. When we read the documents received from Public Safety Canada, the Department of Justice, Industry Canada, and the Canadian Security Intelligence Service (CSIS), as examples, it became evident that domestic "lawful access" surveillance legislation had been an issue predominantly taken up by Public Safety and Justice, and that their publicly stated concern of not being able to rapidly access telecommunications subscriber data had not been borne out in practice (Geist 2013; Parsons 2012). Ultimately, the documents released by the aforementioned federal agencies revealed that the government could not find empirical data demonstrating the need for the legislation, since agents of the government routinely received access to "subscriber data" for use in their investigations.

Moreover, documents released under ATIP show the government's indifference to privacy commissioners' concerns: in one case, the Office of the Privacy Commissioner of Canada (OPC) noted it would lack the resources to conduct audits as envisioned in lawful access legislation. Public Safety Canada noted in internal documents that "the OPC does not receive additional funding every time a government department or agency implements a program that will be subject to OPC review. It is up to every department to determine how best to allocate their resources" (A-2011-00220: 241). Other documents pertaining to surveillance regulations showed that some branches supported the expansion of these regulations whereas others questioned the value of modifying or expanding them. One individual went so far as to ask, "Where is this 'exercise' going? What is its overall purpose? ... the LARGER question is, do we want to go back to the [regulations] ... Do you really want us to re-examine all the standards, etc.; update them to current requirements [...]?" (A-2012-00457: 56). As a result of requesting a broad number of historical ATIP requests, the Citizen Lab was able to evaluate the government's current rationale for such legislation against both past public comments advocating for the legislation and now-public behind-the-scenes concerns about passing the legislation. Aggregating historical ATIP requests can let requesters develop an information "mosaic," whereby reading enough documents beside one another can give a more-or-less comprehensive picture of previous government decisions, debates, or reactions to public protest concerning proposed surveillance legislation.[2]

Historical requests are often helpful not just in providing context about public debates over legislation or government practices that took place while legislation was before the floor or in the media spotlight; they can also reveal issues that demand further public attention. These issues can be researched using either broad or narrow ATIP requests. Broad requests often function as part of exploratory research and are best suited for accessing information about an under-explored, or entirely unexplored, issue. For example, research might involve filing requests to a set of federal agencies asking for copies of policies, correspondence, or policy decisions concerning the collection and use of metadata, or non-content elements of telecommunications, that relate to criminal investigations. The requests could be spurred by public commentary about the importance of metadata for conducting state surveillance in the post-Snowden era (Deibert 2013), or because of the relative *lack* of the term's presence in ATIP requests concerning government surveillance legislation. Is it absent because information about metadata has not been requested before? In the face of such broad requests ATIP staff will attempt to restrict a request to specific kinds of communications, or persons in a communication, or to certain kinds of documents, but they are also obligated to provide assistance in narrowing the request. As a result, these broad requests can lead researchers to large collections of documents that they did not even know existed in the course of liaising with departmental ATIP staff. Narrower requests, in contrast, might focus on accessing specific (and named) policy documents, policy advice, handbooks, or other discrete pieces of information concerning a particular issue. Such requests can often only be made after consultation with an ATIP officer, a leak from a source who is familiar with the information in question, a reference to the document or policy in a ministry's public comments, or a revelation of the document's existence in a previously completed ATIP file. Even narrow requests can be met with lengthy delays if the document is "hard to find," perceived as sensitive in some fashion, or runs afoul of political interference.

Such interference is common in Canada, and often based on three rationales: (i) the requests can be complex; (ii) consultations across government may be needed before disclosing documents; and (iii) communications staff may become deeply involved in "managing" the request (Roberts 2005b). The resolution to such interference begins, first and foremost, with "strong government commitment and political will" to supporting the ATIP regime (Hazell and Worthy 2010: 358). Unfortunately, the 1990s saw the federal government of Canada engage in litigation to restrict how access to information law is interpreted, substantially omit new government institutions from the law, and refine internal processes to ensure the special treatment of "sensitive" requests (Roberts 2005b). Moreover, a 2014 decision by the Supreme Court of Canada may restrict "policy advice" from being accessible under ATIP, with the effect of limiting public knowledge about the creation of new laws, regulations, or policies.[3]

As a result of these legal constraints, and combined with aspects of ATIP legislation meant to "protect" sensitive security- and surveillance-related information, researchers often experience lengthy delays in receiving documents, and what is received is heavily redacted.

It can take years to receive documents and only at great personal time and financial expense, preventing any but the most well-resourced investigators from accessing documents or proceeding through complaints resolution processes. Furthermore, as a result of redactions, what is actually provided can be highly misleading; parts of definitions may be redacted, including terms that have special meaning in law but that are not identified as such. Titles of foundational documents that offer guidance to interpret the documents at hand may also be redacted away. These omissions can cause a reader to misunderstand documents. For example, documents released by the Communications Security Establishment (the Canadian signals intelligence agency) indicated the presence of privacy protections for Canadians while masking the operational limits of such protections (e.g., CSE 2010, 2011). As a result of these limitations to ATIP requests, combined with the often weak powers associated with the federal Information Commissioner responsible for resolving complaints about ATIP processes (Legault 2013; Centre for Law and Democracy 2013), the requesting process can be a slow, onerous, and frustrating way of learning about security and surveillance operations in Canada.

It is in light of these limitations that I urge researchers to adopt an expanded set of methodologies to better understand, and subsequently evaluate and critique, state surveillance programs, policies, and practices.

Facilitating Governmental Accountability

Given that state surveillance practices often intrude upon the private lives of individuals, infringe upon citizens' rights, and threaten democracy, it is incumbent upon researchers to investigate such practices in order to render them more visible to the public (Parsons, Bennett, and Molnar 2015). Such investigations assume heightened importance in Canada for three key reasons: (i) because contemporary surveillance techniques and practices, such as access to emails and text messages, have been kept from statutory reporting requirements (Office of the Privacy Commissioner of Canada 2014); (ii) because surveillance standards have been designed with built-in gag rules preventing companies from informing subscribers if government agencies have requested their information (Kyonka 2014); and (iii) because ministers can authorize new forms of signals intelligence surveillance, such as the capture of metadata anywhere on the Internet, without the public's (or Parliament's) knowledge (Walby and Anaïs 2012). But as mentioned, ATIP requests may not excavate documents quickly enough or with enough unredacted detail to learn about, or prevent, governments from infringing on people's basic rights. In response to deficiencies in the ATIP process, researchers can work with parliamentarians to enhance accountability and, when suspecting overreach or illegal activities, lodge complaints to officers of Parliament and the courts.

Collaboration with Parliamentarians

Sitting opposition parliamentarians are often eager to work with subject matter experts, and enjoy a position of privilege compared to most such experts. In addition to raising national security and surveillance issues onto the political agenda by asking questions in committee meetings and during question period, Members of Parliament have other tools, including the ability to table Order Paper questions. These questions are normally issued when the parliamentarian has a detailed query, or set of queries that are sufficiently technical that a department's minister cannot reasonably be expected to respond to them during question period. Members of Parliament can serve similar, or identical, questions to a set of federal departments simultaneously and the government must provide a response within 45 days. Should the government fail to provide a response within this time frame, the written question is automatically transferred to a standing committee within five days, and the committee is charged with establishing why the government did not respond (Government of Canada 2006).

Order Paper questions can be posed to just one, or all, federal departments and vary in their length and focus. In the case of state surveillance practices, in 2014 MP Charmaine Borg asked the federal government to disclose how, why, and how often federal agencies accessed telecommunications data pertaining to Canadians.[4] Subsequently, other MPs have begun asking related Order Paper questions concerning the magnitude of government access to telecommunications data, the rationales for such requests for access, and the oversight mechanisms in place to evaluate such requests.[5] As a result of MP Borg's inquiry, CSIS, the Royal Canadian Mounted Police (RCMP), Canada Border Services Agency (CBSA), and all other federal security-related departments have provided some information concerning the regularity of and their rationales for accessing Canadians' telecommunications information (Parsons 2014a). Responses from these agencies were revealing. CSIS believed it did not need to respond to the MP's questions, the RCMP revealed the absence of internal reporting procedures, and CBSA provided detailed and aggregate statistics concerning their access and use of privately held telecommunications information.

Although such questions can excavate a wealth of information from government agencies with remarkable speed, working with parliamentarians comes with challenges. First, and perhaps most significantly for research purposes, the sitting member's timetable and the availability of their staff to develop questions with the researcher can be disrupted as new political events arise, or as party whips and staff in the party leader's office issue guidance. As a result, even though responses to questions are received quickly as compared to many ATIP requests, developing and issuing the questions can often take more time than an ATIP request. Second, working with a sitting parliamentarian clearly situates the researchers' inquiries in the formal political domain. Questions placed by a sitting parliamentarian—and especially members of the opposition parties—will necessarily receive heightened political attention since the minister(s) responsible for the responsive departments must be briefed in order to respond to questions that could subsequently arise in Parliament.

Ultimately, while working with a parliamentarian can shift research into the formal political domain, the potential to excavate new data makes this a very promising research method. And, unlike filing complaints or issuing legal challenges, it remains one of the least adversarial means for researchers to collect data on governmental practices and policies, while also working to hold the sitting government to account for its surveillance activities. Though such questions may be regarded as politically motivated when they come from an opposition parliamentarian, there is no direct challenge, on the part of the researcher, to the government's activities (unlike when filing a complaint or challenge).

Complaints and Legal Challenges

Formal complaints brought to parliamentary officers, or legal challenges brought in the courts, provide another way of investigating state surveillance practices. At the same time, these complaints and challenges can hold government to account for existing practices and remediate excessive or outright illegal activities. Given that these processes tend to constitute adversarial challenges between parties, it is typically best that they only be pursued after all other avenues have been exhausted (e.g., ATIP requests, interviews, parliamentary questions, etc.).

The first approach that can be adopted by researchers or advocates to investigate and understand state activities involves bringing a complaint about those activities to independent officers of Parliament. Complaints might be brought to independent bodies about possible breaches of ethics, inappropriate collections of personal information, or the suspect activities of policing organizations. On the issue of state surveillance practices, this approach might entail bringing a complaint to the federal privacy commissioner of Canada, to the office of the communications security establishment commissioner, or oversight bodies for CSIS and the RCMP. Evidence-grounded allegations or concerns can lead commissioners and other oversight bodies to investigate, with the effect of both establishing the legal grounds upon which a federal department bases its surveillance activities, as well as whether such groundings cohere with relevant laws. As an example, such investigations revealed that government departments were operating under the belief that collecting "public" information on citizens is permissible, and thus proceeded to collect information about Canadian activists. The complaint process confirmed that, in fact, indiscriminate collections of public information about Canadians violate the Canadian *Privacy Act* (Office of the Privacy Commissioner of Canada 2013). Alternatively, researchers can privately present findings and concerns to receptive federal or provincial commissioners who may, upon being briefed, launch their own independent investigations that can be wider ranging than when responding to specific complaints or allegations from members of the public.[6] In either case, an investigation can lead to details about government practices that might otherwise be redacted during ATIP processes or "not found" in the course of searching for relevant documents.

Legal challenges are similar to complaints to parliamentary and legislative officers, insofar as they are evidence-based and meant to stop, prevent, or render transparent actions undertaken by the government. However, such challenges demand legal expertise in filing and proceeding through a case, as well as knowledge of how court processes unfold. Where the researcher lacks this expertise it can make sense to partner with non-profits or other groups with the requisite legal experience. The research value of some challenges can be almost immediately apparent. By bringing suit against the government, the researcher and their partners can make evidence-based allegations about what the government is doing and how it infringes on the Charter or other laws. The government's response, in turn, can clarify whether the alleged actions are occurring, underlying legal rationales for those actions, definitions used to "clarify" or legitimize the actions, and so forth. In the UK, this tactic has uncovered details of how signals intelligence agencies understand their mandates as authorizing the indiscriminate collection of information processed through foreign companies' (e.g., Facebook, Google) telecommunications systems (Privacy International 2014). Since late 2013, a series of related challenges have been filed in Canada that aim to both clarify existing federal government surveillance activities and correct surveillance practices that are believed to infringe on Canadians' charter rights.[7]

Complaints to officers of Parliament or challenges brought in court carry a set of risks. First, doing so can prevent ongoing access to members of government to interview. Moreover, when bringing legal challenges against the government it can be difficult, and even inappropriate, to request interviews because an interview might reveal information about the case's legal strategy. Second, adopting these methods transforms the researcher into a very active policy actor, which can lead to allegations of bias in research and publications concerning the complaint and its underlying issues. Moreover, it is possible that taking issues to the courts can cause undesirable policy changes. An example of this is a complaint that went to the Supreme Court of Canada concerning whether policy advice had to be disclosed in ATIP responses. The complainants lost the case, to the effect that government agencies are now not legally required to disclose such advice after receiving an ATIP request.[8] Individual researchers need to judge if these risks—combined with the possible reputation or economic costs if the issue in question is decided in the government's favour—are worth the potential benefit of accessing otherwise inaccessible data in order to affect public policy. Given the seriousness of complaints and especially legal challenges, the researcher should adopt either of these tactics only if they want to change or bring clarity to existing practices. Engaging in complaints or challenges can be incredibly time-consuming and frustrating for all parties involved, and can diminish the complainant's ability to continue with ongoing research pursuits. As such, these tactics should not be engaged in frivolously or without consideration of the costs and risks.

Encouraging Corporate Transparency

Over the course of investigating domestic telecommunications monitoring practices, the Citizen Lab assumed that Canadian telecommunications service providers have been capturing, retaining, and disclosing information to government agencies on the basis of prior research (Parsons 2015). It is less apparent whether such disclosures were voluntary, were predicated on receiving court orders, or were required according to government agencies' statutory powers. And given the prominent role of many Canadian companies in providing information to government agencies, it can be helpful to pressure companies to also render their participation "transparent" to the public. In general, corporate transparency refers to the disclosure of privately held information either by the company's grace or as a result of its obligations. Such obligations "may arise from legal mandate, overriding social pressure, or sufficiently high and public levels of economic self-interest" (Mock 2000). Since telecommunications providers operate as a nexus of Canadians' communications, they are unusually well suited to explain the breadth of the government's telecommunications surveillance activities. However, these companies are not necessarily required to disclose their cooperation with government agencies outside of legal proceedings or parliamentary hearings. In spite of the intractability of these companies to external probing, the Citizen Lab developed a set of methods to simultaneously improve corporate transparency and learn about state surveillance practices.

Detailed Questionnaires

Questionnaires are often best suited for "exploratory" studies, where little is empirically known about a subject area, to establish baseline data sets (Mills 1959; Churchill 1991). One subject area where little is known is the extent to which corporations have been disclosing personal information to governments. Historically, Canadian telecommunications companies have been reluctant to publicly discuss the conditions, rationales, or regularity with which they disclose information about their subscribers to government agencies. These companies are not statutorily required to release such data and, aside from Crown corporations such as Sasktel, are not subject to ATIP laws. In an attempt to elicit this information, the Citizen Lab created and issued detailed questionnaires to each of Canada's largest telecommunications service providers in 2004 (Parsons 2014b). Telecommunications companies were asked to explain their corporate data collection, handling, retention, and disclosure policies, as well as the regularity at which data was disclosed to government and the grounds for such disclosures. Of the eighteen companies that were issued questionnaires, twelve provided marginal responses and five failed to respond at all. Only one company comprehensively responded to the questionnaire (Parsons 2014c).

Issuing the questionnaires has proven to be a useful research strategy, even if most responses have been of limited information value. First, they elicited media attention to specific issues of data handling, and involved television, print, and radio interviews and written commentaries in major Canadian daily newspapers. Such attention was not the goal of the Citizen Lab's public letters though it did put pressure on the companies to explain their practices. Second, they focused on specific practices instead of corporate principles; while such principles matter, they are typically available through corporate websites and do not actually explain the regularity or rationales for providing telecommunications information to state agencies. Third, widespread refusals to respond to even basic questions (e.g., periods for which consumer data information is retained) can be used for subsequent complaints to officers of Parliament which can, in turn, lead to increased disclosure. And fourth, even the companies' limited responses put some additional information into the public domain. The result, in Canada, of a year of sustained investigation into these data handling practices by the Citizen Lab has been that a series of telecommunications companies, including TELUS and TekSavvy, released transparency reports that explain their disclosure of subscribers' data to government agencies. Rogers issued a similar report in the face of public pressure (Freeze, Dobby and Wingrove 2014).

Questionnaires are not without their limitations. Data from respondents can vary widely based on a company's willingness to respond. Moreover, data can be misleading while factually accurate; legal or industry terms may not be interpreted as such by researchers without expert guidance, to the effect of giving one impression when the company "actually" means something else entirely. As well, developing a good questionnaire tends to be a multidisciplinary effort, which means that they can take a long period of time to develop.

Crowdsourcing Right to Information Requests

Questionnaires may produce direct responses to specific questions, but companies are not under any obligation to respond. Businesses operating in Canada are, however, legally required to provide copies of the personal information that they collect or process about Canadian citizens when a citizen requests access to a copy of their data. In Canada, federal commercial law codifies this right and it is (ostensibly) meant to let Canadians learn what data is retained about them in order to subsequently correct false or incorrect records.

In addition to correcting records, Right to Information requests (RTIs) can also be used by researchers to develop an understanding about the kinds of data a company stores about its customers. Learning about industry-wide trends or practices, however, requires a mass of citizens to file similar requests and, ideally, to file at the same time. There are at least two ways of getting such a mass to submit requests: either by directly recruiting individuals or by publicly providing tools to file RTI requests and enabling individuals to submit results to the research team. This latter method is referred to as "crowdsourcing," and amounts to an institution "taking a function once performed by employees and outsourcing it to an undefined (and generally large) network of people in the form of an open call" (Howe 2006).

Researchers at the Citizen Lab developed and released an RTI letter that members of the public could issue to their telecommunications providers. First, a generic template was created and posted on the Citizen Lab website for individuals to download, fill out, and send to their provider(s) (Parsons 2014d). In a subsequent posting, we explained that individuals wanting to issue the requests would need to modify the letter to include their own personal information, as well as either email the completed request or send it by letter mail. Following this, we worked with partners to develop a web app that let Canadians easily and rapidly file requests (Hilts 2014). The app did not collect information on behalf of either the Citizen Lab or our partners, but it did leverage contemporary Internet browser technologies so that completed PDF documents could be printed in order to be mailed or sent to a person's telecommunications provider using the individual's email address (if their provider accepted requests by email). Whereas users of the template letter on the Citizen Lab website had to independently seek out researchers after receiving responses, the web app included an option to be contacted by our outreach partner, Open Media, to share what the telecommunications provider returned in response to the request.

These methods adopted by the Citizen Lab have increased our understanding of what kinds of data are, and are not, retained by telecommunications companies. This includes information about metadata (e.g., whether companies store records of the websites subscribers browse, how long they retain time stamps of text messages), about the content of communications (e.g., retention periods for voicemails, contents of text messages or emails), and about subscriber billing (e.g., how long call records are stored for). In addition, we learned that many Canadian telecommunications companies have interpreted the same commercial privacy law that authorized these requests as "gagging" the companies from stating whether they have, or have not, disclosed subscriber data to government authorities.[9] Finally, responses reveal that the industry does not believe the ability to identify communications data traffic with a subscriber necessarily

makes that data "personal information,"[10] which contrasts with previous assertions of what constitutes such information by the federal
privacy commissioner of Canada (Denham 2009). Most importantly,
these insights are not based on the request of one or two researchers,
but on the responses provided to hundreds of Canadians.

Though there are benefits to this approach to data collection, it
also carries risks. For instance, individuals may receive responses
that they do not understand and ask researchers to clarify company
statements. If this happens on a large scale, it has the potential to be
extremely time-consuming. Also, data cannot be positively verified
if individuals do not share primary documents (and, if such documents are shared, researchers must carefully manage the personally
identifiable information). Moreover, in working with multiple partners (non-profits, outreach partners, activist organizations) there
can be challenging negotiations concerning what semi-automated
RTI tools or web apps are meant to accomplish, and how resulting
data can or should be mobilized.

Ultimately, RTI requests and questionnaires are unlikely, on their
own, to explain how or why government agencies are accessing
company data sources. But insights into corporate data collection,
retention, and processing practices can indicate the kinds of government access requests that are more or less likely; that is, companies
with long data retention schedules or excessive data mining practices might receive different kinds of court orders for data (such as
for historical data or access to mined data) than those with short retention schedules or more limited subscriber data processing. When
this information is combined with knowledge of government practices unearthed by ATIPs, complaints, or whistle-blowing, then state
surveillance practices and rationales for accessing particular kinds
of data can be rendered more transparent.

Complaints to Parliamentary Officers
Researchers can both learn about corporate practices as well as potentially change them by filing complaints to federal ombudspersons

or commissioners. Through this strategy, companies may be pressured to reveal in more depth the kinds of data that they disclose to government agencies, the regularity at which data is disclosed, and the rationales for such disclosures. They can also be pressured into publishing data collection, retention, and processing practices. Such complaints might be mounted using the "Openness" principle of federal privacy law, which maintains that an "organization shall make readily available to individuals specific information about its policies and practices relating to the management of personal information." Complaints can be made on the grounds that telecommunications companies are unsatisfactorily responding to RTI requests or, alternatively, that they are obligated to provide "transparency reports" that explain to consumers how often government agencies request and receive company information. Moreover, where companies' actions appear to contradict regulations that they must adhere to as a condition of providing services, their actions could be challenged before other agencies such as the federal telecommunications regulator.

Complaints to parliamentary officers and regulators have been effective, in the past, in learning about telecommunications companies' surveillance activities and placing restrictions on corporate behaviour (Denham 2009; Parsons 2013). However, like the other research strategies documented in this chapter, complaints are also associated with certain risks. Perhaps the most obvious risk is that the researcher might lose access to corporate representatives during the complaint process. And as with filing complaints against government, bringing complaints to an officer of parliament or regulator establishes the researcher as an involved policy actor, not "merely" a policy researcher. Furthermore, the parliamentary officer or regulator might come to a conclusion that the researcher opposes; by bringing forward a complaint, a practice that is distasteful to the researcher might be legitimized by government agencies that are independent of Parliament. Given the seriousness of some of these risks, to say nothing of the time and effort involved in preparing and filing strong complaints, researchers should adopt this tactic only if they are first and foremost interested in changing or rendering transparent a corporate practice, and not simply because they want to access otherwise unavailable research data.

New Methods and New Data

While this chapter has been written in the context of state surveillance, the methods outlined here can be repurposed to investigate many other government policies and practices. Regardless of the issue investigated, the combination of improved accountability and transparency can provide new sources of research data while also potentially remediating inappropriate, unjust, unconstitutional, and undemocratic government and corporate practices.

Indeed, the research strategies discussed here have already been influential in changing government and corporate behaviour. In terms of corporate transparency, for example, citizens can now request copies of the information that telecommunications providers retain about them. Transparency reports, which describe the sharing of subscriber information with governments, are becoming more common in the telecommunications sector. As a result of ongoing pressure, the Minister of Industry Canada has formally declared that companies are authorized to produce these reports.[11] I also suspect that complaints currently being made to the office of the privacy commissioner of Canada concerning the inadequate responses to RTI letters may improve how companies disclose information to subscribers in the future. In terms of government accountability, questions raised by parliamentarians have revealed insights into the practices of CSIS, CBSA, and the RCMP, and have led to ongoing debates concerning the magnitude and legitimacy of state surveillance practices. Legal challenges are in their earliest stages but, based on telecommunications-related decisions by the Supreme Court of Canada,[12] appear promising in their capacity to remediate undemocratic government surveillance practices (Parsons, Israel and Vonn 2014).

Using the methods discussed in this chapter can uncover a wealth of hidden data and information, which can then be used to foster changes in the way that corporations and governments operate. None of these methods can replace the ATIP process, but ATIP alone is insufficient to learn about, understand, and challenge many current policies and practices. Therefore, it is imperative for researchers to move beyond ATIP-only research strategies when investigating pressing issues of governance and social justice.

NOTES

1   *Dagg v. Canada (Minister of Finance)*, 1997 2 S.C.R. 403.
2   This "mosaic theory of state secrets" is routinely used to avoid disclosing "seemingly insignificant data on grounds that sufficient amounts of disclosures would in aggregate endanger national security." See: Weaver, W. and R. Pallitto. 2005. State Secrets and Executive Power. *Political Science* 120(1): 104.
3   *John Doe v. Ontario (Finance)*, 2014 SCC 36.
4   Q-233 and Q-234, <parl.gc.ca/HousePublications/Publication.aspx?Language=E&Mode=1&Parl=41&Ses=2&DocId=6391359&File=11>
5   Q-511, <parl.gc.ca/HousePublications/Publication.aspx?Pub=Notice Order&Mode=1&Language=E&Parl=41&Ses=2&File=9&Col=1>
6   Based on discussions with members of the Office of the Information and Privacy Commissioner for British Columbia, 2012-2013.
7   *British Columbia Civil Liberties Association v. Attorney General of Canada*; Corporation of the *Canadian Civil Liberties Association & Christopher Parsons v. Attorney General of Canada* (CV-14-504139).
8   *John Doe v. Ontario (Finance)*, 2014 SCC 36.
9   Personal correspondence between Christopher Parsons and Chet Patel, Advisor to Rogers' Office of the President, July 1, 2014; similar responses have been provided by Fido and TELUS.
10 Based on correspondence between Andrew Hilts and Fido Communications, summer 2014.
11 Hon. James Moore. 2014. Government correspondence to Tamir Israel, July 24, 2014.
12 *R. v. Spencer*, 2014 SCC 43.

REFERENCES

Birkinshaw, P. 2006. Freedom of Information and Openness: Fundamental Human Rights? *Administrative Law Review* 58(1): 177-218.

Centre for Law and Democracy. January 2013. Response to the OIC Call for Dialogue: Recommendations for Improving the Right to Information in Canada. At <oic-ci.gc.ca/eng/modernization-atia_2012_all-submissions-tous-soumissions.aspx>

Churchill, G. A. 1991. *Marketing Research: Methodological Foundations* (5th ed.). Orlando: Dryden Press.

Communications Security Establishment (CSE). 2011. Ministerial Directive Communications Security Establishment Collection and Use of Metadata. Released under CSE ATIP A-2012-00776. November 21.

_____. 2010. OPS-1, Protecting the Privacy of Canadians and Ensuring the legal Compliance in the Conduct of CSEC Activities. Released under CSE ATIP. December 1.

Deibert, R. 2013. Spy Agencies have Turned Our Lives Inside Out. We Need to Watch Them. *The Globe and Mail*, June 11.

Denham, E. September 2009. PIPEDA Case Summary #2009-010. At <priv.gc.ca/cf-dc/2009/2009_010_rep_0813_e.asp>

Freeze, C, C. Dobby and J. Wingrove. 2014. TekSavvy, Rogers Break Silence over Government Requests for Data. *The Globe and Mail*, June 5.

Geist, M. 2013. Lawful Access is Dead (For Now): Government Kills Bill C-13. February 12. At <michaelgeist.ca/2013/02/bill-c-30-dead/>

Government of Canada. 2006. Order Paper-Questions. At <parl.gc.ca/About/House/compendium/web-content/c_d_orderpaperquestions-e.htm>

Hazell, R. and B. Worthy. 2010. Assessing the Performance of Freedom of Information. *Government Information Quarterly* 27(4): 352-359.

Hilts, A. 2014. Access Your Info with the AMI Tool. At <digitalstewards.ca/tools/access-my-info/>

Howe, J. 2006. Crowdsourcing: A Definition. At <crowdsourcing.typepad.com/cs/2006/06/crowdsourcing_a.html>

Kyonka, N. 2014. Rules Could Stymie Inquiry of Telecoms' Info Disclosure to Government. At <thewirereport.ca/news/2014/02/10/rules-could-stymie-inquiry-of-telecoms%E2%80%99-info-disclosure-to-government/27839>

Legault, S. 2013. Speaking Notes of Suzanne Legault Information Commissioner of Canada to the Canadian Legal Information Institute (CanLII) Conference. September 13. At <oic-ci.gc.ca/eng/media-room-salle-media_speeches-discours_2013_5.aspx>

Mills, C. W. 1959. *The Sociological Imagination*. New York: Oxford University Press.

Mock, W. B. T. 2000. Corporate Transparency and Human Rights. *Tulsa Journal of Comparative and International Law* 8(1): 15-26.

Office of the Privacy Commissioner of Canada. 2014. Checks and Controls: Reinforcing Privacy Protection and Oversight for the Canadian Intelligence Community in an Era of Cyber-Surveillance. At <priv.gc.ca/information/sr-rs/201314/sr_cic_e.asp#section6-1>

_____. 2013. Aboriginal Affairs and Northern Development Canada Wrongly Collects Information from First Nations Activist's Personal Facebook Page. At <priv.gc.ca/cf-dc/pa/2012-13/pa_201213_01_e.asp>

_____. 2009. PIPEDA Case Summary #2009-008 Report of Findings into the Complaint Filed by the Canadian Internet Policy and Public Interest Clinic (CIPPIC) against Facebook Inc. Under the *Personal Information Protection and Electronic Documents Act*. At <priv.gc.ca/cf-dc/2009/2009_008_0716_e.asp>

Parsons, C. (Forthcoming). Stuck on the Agenda: Drawing Lessons from the Stagnation of 'Lawful Access' Legislation in Canada. In M. Geist and W. Wark (eds.), *Law, Privacy and Surveillance in Canada in a Post-Snowden Era*. Ottawa: University of Ottawa Press.

_____. 2014a. Mapping the Canadian Government's Telecommunications Surveillance. At <citizenlab.org/2014/03/mapping-canadian-governments-telecommunications-surveillance/>

_____. 2014b. Towards Transparency in Canadian Telecommunications. At <citizenlab.org/2014/01/towards-transparency-canadian-telecommunications/>

_____. 2014c. The Murky State of Canadian Telecommunications Surveillance. At <citizenlab.org/2014/03/murky-state-canadian-telecommunications-surveillance/>

_____. 2014d. Responding to the Crisis in Canadian Telecommunications. At <citizenlab.org/2014/05/responding-crisis-canadian-telecommunications/>

_____. 2013. The Politics of Deep Packet Inspection: What Drives Contemporary Western Internet Service Provider Surveillance Practices? At <christopher-parsons.com/Academic/Parsons_Christopher_PhD_2013.pdf>

_____. 2012. Canadian Social Media Surveillance: Today and Tomorrow. At <christopher-parsons.com/canadian-social-media-surveillance-today-and-tomorrow/>

Parsons, C., C. Bennett and A. Molnar. (Forthcoming). Privacy, Surveillance, and the Democratic Potential of the Social Web. In B. Roessler and D. Mokrosinska (eds.), *The Social Dimensions of Privacy*. Cambridge: Cambridge University Press.

Parsons, C., T. Israel and M. Vonn. 2014. A Crisis of Accountability: A Global Analysis of the Impact of the Snowden Revelations. In S. Davies (ed.). At <citizenlab.org/wp-content/uploads/2014/06/Snowden-final-report-for-publication.pdf>

Parsons, C., C. Bennett and A. Molnar. 2015. Privacy, Surveillance, and the Democratic Potential of the Social Web. In B. Roessler and D. Mokrosinska (eds.), *The Social Dimensions of Privacy*. Cambridge: Cambridge University Press.

Privacy International. 2014. UK Intelligence Forced to Reveal Secret Policy for Mass Surveillance of Residents' Facebook and Google Use. At <privacyinternational.org/press-releases/uk-intelligence-forced-to-reveal-secret-policy-for-mass-surveillance-of-residents>

Roberts, A. 2005a. Transparency in the Security Sector. In A. Florini (ed.), *The Right to Know: Transparency for an Open World*. New York: Columbia University Press.

_____. 2005b. Spin Control and Freedom of Information: Lessons for the United Kingdom from Canada. *Public Administration* 83(1): 1-23.

Walby, K. and S. Anaïs. 2012. Communications Security Establishment Canada (CSEC), Structures of Secrecy, and Ministerial Authorization after September 11. *Canadian Journal of Law and Society* 27(3): 363-380.

HELPFUL TIPS FROM FREQUENT ATI/FOI USERS

Dean Jobb

TIP #1

To avoid search and processing fees as well as delays, be as specific as possible when describing the records sought.

TIP #2

To make sure nothing has been omitted and to see if follow-up requests are needed to unearth related records, carefully read every document released.

TIP #3

Don't take "no" for an answer. Appeal any refusal to release all or part of an important record. It's the best way to expand access rights and keep the system honest.

Leslie Young

TIP #1

Never. Stop. Calling. Sometimes (okay, a lot of the time) your request will be delayed. Maybe they lost it. Maybe they don't know what you're asking for. Or maybe they don't want to give it to you. You won't know unless you call. If it's late, call and find out why. Complain to the information commissioner if you don't like the answers.

TIP #2

Don't take "no" for an answer. There is always room for negotiation. If the government is concerned about privacy, figure out a way to get the information you want without compromising privacy, like disguising addresses with the first three letters of a postal code, or removing columns from a table. Be creative.

TIP #3

If you asked for data, don't accept it as a PDF. You can't analyze them, you can hardly read them, and in some cases you can't even copy and paste them. Sometimes you will lose this battle, but you should fight it anyway. Worst case, Optical Character Recognition programs can work wonders on a PDF (though slowly and painfully).

Jeffrey Monaghan

TIP #1

There are no "stupid" questions. Assume that federal ATI officers are not aware of particular programs, acronyms, policies, etc. Always take the opportunity to ask questions about how bureaucracies work, and what may or may not be happening in particular government departments or offices.

TIP #2

Stay on top of files. Keep precise records on your end. Send queries when files are coming up late. Track redaction/exemption sections.

TIP #3

Try informal requests. Federal departments post monthly lists of disclosed ATIs. You can check these lists online and make informal requests for those files. These can be done for free and are usually processed quickly. Although they may not give you the information you're looking for, they can be useful for identifying key groups, teams, employees, programs, and funds.

Keith Stewart and Kyla Tanner

TIP #1

Use the lobbyist registry to identify meetings between industry representatives and federal officials or politicians. Then focus your requests on the documents related to those meetings.

TIP #2

Use the federal government's online Government Electronic Directory Services to identify the civil servant(s) working on a file you are interested in. Then request any memos or reports that they have helped to prepare.

TIP #3

Talk to your ATI officer about how to refine your request. Some (not all) are very helpful.

Franke James

TIP #1

Make dumb information smart again. Bureaucrats are paid to turn "smart" digital records into "dumb" scanned images. This makes them hard to share, and even harder to search. The first thing to do when you get an ATI release is undo their "dumb" efforts. Scan the entire package to create a digital file. Then use OCR software (e.g., Adobe Acrobat's optical character recognition software) to turn the scanned documents into searchable text. Being able to search by keyword and copy text will be invaluable to you as you read, analyze, and annotate the documents.

TIP #2

Be nakedly transparent. Exposure for "saying one thing while doing another" is why all levels of government are afraid of transparency. Tear away their veil of secrecy by posting digital ATI files on the web. (Scribd is used by many info-warriors and journalists to post ATI files.) Don't forget to tag the bureaucrats. Tweet and share on social media. Tape all your phone calls so you can respond back with call reports to document what was said.

TIP #3

Be tenacious and skeptical. The simple truth is that some government agencies don't want to give you the information. But don't give up. ATI officers may send you letters indicating that no records exist. At that point, revisit your documents. Ask yourself if their refusal passes the smell test. Create a timeline of communications to help you spot where the holes are. If you have reasonable grounds to object to their refusal, fire off complaints.

Alex Luscombe and Michael-Anthony Lutfy

TIP #1

It is not just about "the dirt." Mundane or "ordinary" records can be equally informative about the actions and decisions of governments. Mundane accounts often reveal how agencies *think*, so take them seriously.

TIP #2

Angles are everything. Mix ATI requests with other sources of data, whether it be newspaper articles, government publications, interviews, or observations from the field. This can provide a more holistic view and it also avoids privileging ATI disclosures in isolation.

TIP #3

Resist the temptation to jump to conclusions when analyzing government records. ATI documents tell us as much about what we don't know as what we do know.

Justin Piché

TIP #1

Simplify your research findings. Clearly identify and describe the key pieces of information you receive, especially for those who may be unfamiliar with the issues and/or the ATI process.

TIP #2

Identify target audiences and communicate your research findings. Compile a contact list of individuals and groups whose work might be affected and/or informed by the information you receive. Take stock of the tactics that most effectively communicate your findings to target audiences.

TIP #3

Analyze communication outcomes. Keep track of the impact that the communication of your research findings is having (e.g., in media commentary and political debates) and use this to inform subsequent communication and outreach.

Christopher Parsons

TIP #1

Before filing your request, look through previously completed requests. Review those linked with what you're interested in. Then, when you file your own request, you'll be able to catch and push back on agencies that recycle previously disclosed documents instead of searching for new documents that might better pertain to your request.

TIP #2

Previously completed ATI requests often contain data that has not been publicly reported, despite its newsworthiness. Long-form articles and series-based articles can often be fleshed out by mining for these previously unreported gems of information.

TIP #3

Access to information may not always be the right avenue to get the data you are seeking. Don't be afraid or unwilling to experiment with different options, such as working with Members of Parliament to draft and issue Order Paper questions.

CONTRIBUTORS

JAMIE BROWNLEE completed his PhD in sociology and political economy at Carleton University, where he currently teaches and conducts research in the areas of Canadian and international political economy, corporate crime, environmental politics and climate change, and the sociology of education. He is the author of *Ruling Canada: Corporate Cohesion and Democracy* (Fernwood 2005), which explores how Canada's economic elite cooperate to control state and national policy. He recently published *Academia, Inc.: How Corporatization is Transforming Canadian Universities* (Fernwood 2015), which examines the influence of corporate power in the sphere of higher education. The book draws on Brownlee's original access to information research on casualized academic labour in Ontario. Brownlee's work has also appeared in journals such as *Higher Education, Organization & Environment,* and *Paedagogica Historica.*

ROBERT CRIBB is an award-winning investigative reporter at the *Toronto Star.* He has received national reporting awards and citations for investigations into child exploitation, human trafficking, dangerous doctors, and public health threats and has received the Massey Journalism Fellowship, the Atkinson Fellowship in Public Policy Reporting, and the Michener-Deacon Fellowship. Cribb is past president of the Canadian Association of Journalists, current president of the CAJ's Educational Foundation, and co-author of *Digging Deeper: A Canadian Reporter's Research Guide* (Oxford University Press). He teaches investigative reporting at Ryerson University's School of Journalism and the University of Toronto.

FRANKE JAMES is a Canadian artist, author, and activist who draws inspiration from the Canadian government's attempts to silence her. In *Banned on the Hill: A True Story about Dirty Oil and Government Censorship* (2013), James describes how she discovered she was being censured for her role in speaking out on climate change and the Alberta tar sands—and how she fought back. In 2015, James won the inaugural PEN Canada/Ken Filkow Prize for showing courage and integrity in the interest of freedom of expression. In 2014, the BC Civil Liberties Association presented James with its Excellence in the Arts award for her creative fight for free expression and social justice. *Banned on the Hill* has been recognized by winning Gold at the 2014 Independent Book Publishers Awards, a Silver at the IndieFab Book of the Year Awards, and Gold at the 2015 eLit Awards. James is also the author of two other books, *Bothered by My Green Conscience* (2009) and *Dear Office-Politics* (2009).

DEAN JOBB is an associate professor in the School of Journalism at the University of King's College in Halifax. He is the author of *Media Law for Canadian Journalists*, 2nd ed. (Emond Montgomery Publications 2011) and co-author of *Digging Deeper: A Canadian Reporter's Research Guide*, 3rd ed. (Oxford University Press 2015). An award-winning writer and journalist, he has published six other books including *Empire of Deception: From Chicago to Nova Scotia – The Incredible Story of a Master Swindler Who Seduced a City and Captivated the Nation* (HarperCollins Canada 2015). Jobb is the former freedom of information and protection of privacy officer for King's College. He also chaired an advisory committee that reviewed Nova Scotia's *Freedom of Information and Protection of Privacy Act.*

MICHAEL-ANTHONY LUTFY completed his undergraduate degree in criminology with a concentration in forensic psychology and is currently pursuing a Master of Arts in the Department of Law & Legal Studies at Carleton University. His research interests include the policing and regulation of dissent, social movements, security-intelligence, and continental philosophy. Currently, Lufty is experimenting with sustainable indoor and outdoor urban vegetable gardening.

ALEX LUSCOMBE is a Master of Arts candidate in the Department of Sociology and Anthropology at Carleton University. His research interests include military sociology, criminology, and law. His SSHRC-funded Master's research, which incorporates records released under the United States' *Freedom of Information Act*, investigates strategies of public deception in an Anglo-American Cold War intelligence operation. Luscombe's work has been published in the *Canadian Journal of Criminology and Criminal Justice*, where he used access to information disclosures to research the policing of Occupy Ottawa, and in *Police Practice & Research: An International Journal*, where he assessed the usefulness of access to information requests for research on national security agencies. His work also appears in *Municipal Corporate Security in International Context* (Routledge 2015).

JEFFREY MONAGHAN teaches criminology in Ottawa. As a frequent user of the *Access to Information Act*, he has published on a wide range of contemporary issues related to policing and security practices in academic journals such as *Policing and Society*, the *Canadian Journal of Law and Society*, *Current Sociology*, *Security Dialogue*, and *Surveillance and Society*. Combining ATI research with security expert interviews, his PhD research examined the export of Canadian policing and security practices abroad. Monaghan's chapter in this volume represents a reflection on the hundreds of ATI requests he filed during the course of his dissertation research.

CHRISTOPHER PARSONS received his Bachelor's and Master's degrees from the University of Guelph, and his PhD from the University of Victoria. He is currently a Postdoctoral Fellow at the Citizen Lab in the Munk School of Global Affairs at the University of Toronto, as well as Managing Director of the Telecom Transparency Project at the Citizen Lab. His research focuses on how privacy is affected by digitally mediated surveillance, and the normative implications that corporate and government surveillance has in (and on) Western political systems. Parsons is currently investigating the rationales, practices, and politics of third-party access to telecommunications data. In addition to academic publishing, he routinely presents his findings to members of the government and the media. He is also a Privacy by Design Ambassador and a Principal at Block G Privacy and Security Consulting.

JUSTIN PICHÉ is an assistant professor in the Department of Criminology at the University of Ottawa and managing editor of the *Journal of Prisoners on Prisons*. Piché has used access to information research to expose the Conservative government's crime and punishment agenda, and mobilize and circulate information about new prison capacity expansion in Canada. His current research explores carceral expansion and abolitionist alternatives in the Canadian context, public criminology and social movements, and cultural representations of confinement and punishment in penal history museums. Recent publications include a chapter in *Brokering Access: Power, Politics, and Freedom of Information Process in Canada* (2012) and articles in the *Canadian Journal of Law and Society* (2011), *Penal Field* (2014), and *Social Justice* (2015).

KEITH STEWART leads Greenpeace Canada's climate and energy campaign, which is focused on stopping the expansion of the tar sands and accelerating the transition away from fossil fuels by building an equitable and sustainable energy system. He holds a PhD in political science from York University and is currently a part-time faculty member at the University of Toronto where he teaches on energy policy and the environment. Stewart has worked as an energy policy analyst and advocate for the last sixteen years, including on successful campaigns to phase out coal-fired power plants and enact a green energy act in Ontario.

KYLA TANNER is a graduate student at York University where she is completing her Master's degree in Environmental Studies. Her work focuses on environmental policy and she is currently conducting research on how the Canadian news media reports on federal climate change policy decisions. Tanner is a volunteer with Greenpeace Canada and eMERGE Guelph, and has worked as a policy analyst with the Commissioner of Environment and Sustainable Development and Environment Canada in Ottawa.

KEVIN WALBY is an associate professor and Chancellor's Research Chair in the Department of Criminal Justice at the University of Winnipeg. He is the author of *Touching Encounters: Sex, Work, and Male-for-Male Internet Escorting* (University of Chicago Press 2012). He is a co-editor of *Emotions Matter: A Relational Approach to Emotions* with A. Hunt and D. Spencer (University of Toronto Press 2012) and *Brokering Access: Power, Politics, and Freedom of Information Process in Canada* with M. Larsen (UBC Press 2012). He has co-edited with R.K. Lippert *Policing Cities: Urban Securitization and Regulation* (Routledge 2013) and *Corporate Security in the 21st Century: Theory and Practice in International Perspective* (Palgrave 2014). Walby is also co-author with R.K. Lippert of *Municipal Corporate Security in International Context* (Routledge 2015) and the Prisoners' Struggles editor for the *Journal of Prisoners on Prisons*.

LESLIE YOUNG is a Canadian investigative and data journalist. Her written work has appeared in the *Vancouver Sun*, *The Globe and Mail*, *Zeit Online*, and *Global News*, and her television and radio stories on CBC Radio and PBS. She has won local and national awards for investigative and digital reporting as well as an Emmy Award for best investigative feature in a television news magazine. Young has reported from sewage plants in Vancouver, Parliament Hill in Ottawa, a refugee camp in Jordan, and villages in the former East Germany. She currently works for *Global News* in Toronto, writing news stories and creating interactive features for their website.

ACKNOWLEDGEMENTS

Jamie and Kevin would like to acknowledge the tremendous support of their families, friends, and colleagues, as well as the hard work and dedication of all the authors in this volume. Many thanks also to Josina Robb, Peter Ives, and everyone else at ARP Books. All royalties from the sale of this collection will be donated to the Old Market Autonomous Zone in Winnipeg.